"Most people know Frederick Marx from Hoop Dreams, Journey From Zanskar, and other fine films. They probably don't know that he is a longtime student of dharma, an ordained Zen priest, and a gifted writer exploring the terrain of the human heart. This book shivers with the frailties of what it means to be human, enfolding loss in all its forms, finding a way through acceptance and the pure ground of being back to love."

—Ram Dass, author of Be Here Now

"This book is one's man's story of love, loss, and realization; actually it is a story that many of us know or will know. Heartbreaking, beautiful, intimate, challenging… this is a book we should all read."

—Rev. Joan Jiko Halifax

"Frederick Marx has written a touchingly intimate account of love, loss and healing. Losing a loved one is something most everyone faces at some point in life. At Death Do Us Part shows the possibility of navigating through this journey with consciousness, understanding and an open-heart."

—James Baraz, co-author of Awakening Joy: 10 Steps to Happiness; co-founding teacher Spirit Rock Meditation Center, Woodacre, California

"Raw and beautiful, this tender, joyous look into the shared intimacy of a mature couple, seems almost too secret to put into words. I felt touched so many times in so many ways by this unique wisdom-teaching. As I slowly read the book, I kept falling in love with Frederick. His utterly fearless transparency constantly endeared him to me."

—Bill Kauth, co-founder of The ManKind Project; co-author of A Circle of Men and We Need Each Other

"At Death Do Us Part is a book about life, of change, of opening your heart. Reading Frederick's words and mulling over his stories, I feel that my world is now filled with more depth and more flavors, as well as some new questions and insights about this thing we call being alive. A beautiful, moving book."

—Marc Lesser, author of Less: Accomplishing More By Doing Less

"I was deeply moved by Frederick's story beginning with the words from his introduction. 'How do you get over losing your life partner?' This is an experience none of us want to go through, yet it is one that is part of the inevitable human journey. Frederick offers us a glimpse into our present and future losses, but does it in such a beautiful and caring way, we feel like we're with a true guide and loving friend who is holding us in his kind embrace."

—Jed Diamond, author My Distant Dad: Healing the Family Father Wound

"How to express how deeply I am touched by this remarkable tale of the truth of living and dying? This is not just an autobiography and history of [their] time together and its cancerous ending, but also a Buddhist dharma teaching. Life and death lived within the Buddhist perspective. It is gift from them to and for all of us. We all need to come to compassionate understanding and radical acceptance of the truth of dying. This book is a great sharing teaching of this understanding."

—JunPo Denis Kelly, Abbot of the Hollow Bones Order of Rinzai Zen

"I have always been aware of Frederick's brilliance, so easy to see in his important documentaries. Now he takes that brilliance once again through the portals of his heart, to share a very intimate, soul-searching book of loss and grief… and beauty and love. All of which can be found in his cracked open heart upon the death of his wife."

—Meredith Little, author & founder of School of Lost Borders

"It's surprisingly enjoyable, moving, captivating, engrossing. Marx revives-reanimates-re-loves–his partner–not as saint, but as person–with textured, reverent, and humorous delight, showing that grief is not a one way trip to a lugubrious terminus but a single stop on a vast, circuitous journey, a dizzying, dazzling topography filled with aliveness, presence, love."

—Jiwon Chung

"Just like Frederick I've been lost. Like him, Buddhist meditation changed my fundamental perspective on how to approach life, how to deal with failure. There's a level beyond understanding on offer here… Frederick knows that there's a time when being out of integrity, out of wholeness, our internal sense of good, becomes too great a pain for a man to carry. Like other good men, he has that strong internal compass to guide that pull back to being the man he knows he can be."

—Rich Tosi, co-founder of The ManKind Project; co-founder of A Couples Weekend

"At Death Do Us Part is a beautiful testament and memorial to an extraordinary woman through deep realizations of love and relationship. The experience of reading At Death Do Us Part reminds me of a Buddhist, "bare bones," practice of just showing up for what is, with no place to hide. This is not an easy read; yet, it is an important undertaking that evokes within the reader the courage that was necessary to share this narrative."

Dr. Timothy P Dukes, author, The Present Parent Handbook.

AT DEATH DO US PART

At Death Do Us Part

A Grieving Widower Heals After Losing his Wife to Breast Cancer

FREDERICK MARX

© 2018 Frederick Marx

CONTENTS

Introduction 1
Chapter 1 3
Chapter 2 19
Chapter 3 43
Chapter 4 81
Chapter 5 107
Chapter 6 139
Chapter 7 149
Chapter 8 173
Chapter 9 195
Thank You 221
Acknowledgements 223
About the Author 225
My Final Prayer 227

"VIDA VIVIDA"

Go back, life I have lived
So I can see again

Go back, life I have lived
So I can see again

That life lost
That I never knew how to live

That life lost
That I never knew how to live

To go back again I wish
To that time. How I miss it

To return again I wish
To that time. How I miss it

Spring always returns
Only innocence does not

Spring always returns
Only innocence does not

Time goes by
And we delude ourselves

Time goes by
And we delude ourselves

Laughing, crying
Crying, laughing

Laughing, crying
Crying, laughing

My God how time flies
We sometimes say

My God how time flies
We sometimes say

After all, time stands still
We are the ones passing through

After all, time stands still
We are the ones passing through

written by Joao de Freitas and Filipe de Almelda Pinto
sung by Argentina Santos
in the film "Fados" by Carlos Saura

INTRODUCTION

How do you get over losing your life partner? Your soul mate? Where does that leave your soul? If you know the mate you had was the ideal one for you, that there could be no other, certainly no better, what does that say about your future? Do I spend the rest of my life mourning, feeling half-complete? Do I become a ghost myself, half alive? Walking this earth in grief and tribute to one gone? What kind of life is that? I'd rather be dead.

CHAPTER 1
WERNER MARX
MAY 9, 1923—FEB. 3, 1965

TRACY'S DEAD. I have to say the words to myself many times a day so I can begin to believe it.

Knowing that death is coming does little to mitigate against the impact of its arrival. Like hearing the sound of a distant train whistle. You're vaguely aware a train is coming. Only too late do you look up and see it bearing down when you suddenly realize you're standing on the tracks. There's no way to anticipate or prepare for that moment, the one that forever divides before from after.

She is with you. Everything you say and do is part of a conversation. There is another; your beloved is present; you are in relationship. Consciousness has circularity and reciprocity. It cycles from one to the other and back again. Then suddenly it does not. There is no other. You are alone. You are talking to yourself. And it literally happens in one second. The definitiveness is overwhelming. You are impaled by the sharp clarity of that one insurmountable difference. You have crossed over from "our time together" to "forever apart." There is no going back. In an instant day becomes night and will not return.

The physical feeling is unforgettable. It was like having my stomach squeezed from the inside. Pressure, inescapable tightening. For the first time in my entire life other than illness I had no appetite and took no joy in food. For almost the first time I couldn't sleep. The first days I'd awaken between 4:15 and 4:27—the echoing moment of her death. I was lucky if I could sleep steadily for two straight hours. Now as I write this, one month later, I still wake up 2-3 nights each week at that time. At least I don't sob now. I meditate and fall back asleep.

I was and still am so grateful that I was awake and by her side as she passed. She lay in a portable hospital bed in our bedroom two feet from where I slept on what had been the bed we shared for 13 years. At around midnight the quality of her breathing shifted to something more raspy. She was still able to easily swallow the 2ml of Haldol I squirted into her mouth. At around 2 am she started sighing and slightly moaning at times so I gave her 1ml of oxycodone. That seemed to work and quieted her. I gave her another 2ml of Haldol at 4 am. After I lay back down I started feeling guilty for not checking her diaper. Then at 4:15 her breathing got more gurgly. I didn't know if she'd swallowed the Haldol. I think she had but I worried it had collected in her throat. So I gave her 1ml of oxycodone to help her breathing. That for sure she may never have swallowed. But I raised the head of her bed to help her breathe more easily. The gurgling continued so I sat beside her stroking her forearm. Then she opened her eyes pretty wide and immediately half closed them.

Then came a big exhale. It wasn't her final breath. There was more gurgling and foam was collecting on the left side of her mouth, between her lips. Her half-closed eyes were glassy. Then she took what turned out to be her final last small breath or two. I spoke after or just before those final breaths, the only words that came to mind: *Go in love. Go in light.* I realized she stopped breathing but checked by (stupidly) holding my hand to her nostrils. (She'd been exclusively mouth-breathing for at least 24 hours.) It must've been then that I noticed a tear on her cheek. As she was leaning slightly to her left side it had escaped her left eye and was sitting on her cheek. A tear of sadness? Of final farewell? Of fluid build-up in that eye? Who knows? But I found it so deeply touching, so perfectly Tracy.

I will wonder for the rest of my life what Tracy saw just before her final breath, when she suddenly opened wide her eyes. They had been closed for some hours. She seemed startled. She was staring straight ahead at the makeshift altar I created, candles burning. But I doubt she saw that. The portal to the other world opening wide? The white light people talk about? Her mother and, possibly, even her father opening their arms to greet her? What awaited her when she passed through that gate?

And I ask myself now, why didn't I kiss her one last time?

I WAS NINE years old when my dad died, and I didn't get to witness his final moments. It was 16 years before I knew all that actually happened to him. When I got home from school that day right away I knew something was different. Two of my father's college students were holding each other on the living room couch. They seemed startled to see me. My child mind made up the story that I caught them necking and they were embarrassed. The male student told me solemnly, "Your mother wants to see you in the bedroom."

I walked into her room. She was working at the little desk in the corner, by the windows. I stepped toward her. She turned and said, "Fred, your Dad is dead." I don't remember saying anything, maybe "oh." She might've said more. Maybe she said, "He died of a heart attack." But what I remember is her turning back to the work on her desk. "I guess it's time for me to leave," I thought. I walked into the bedroom I shared with my brother Larry who was four. He was sitting on the floor playing a game with our family friend Ruth Lorbe. He looked up brightly, "Hey Fred, did you hear Dad is dead?" "Yeah," I said, and walked out. It was only then I remember hearing my 11-year-old sister crying behind the closed door of her bedroom. I looked into the living room and saw the student couple "necking." Maybe they looked forlornly at me. I don't know. They were probably consoling each other. What I suddenly did know was that there was no place for me to be alone.

I went to the only place left in our house where I could close the door, to be alone with my confusion. I went to the bathroom. I put the toilet lid down and sat. "What does this mean?" I couldn't wrap my head around it. I listened to my sister crying across the hall. My agitation bloomed. I needed someplace to be. I felt stupid sitting in the bathroom on the toilet. I didn't want to be there but I had to be somewhere. But where? The restlessness in my body needed some place to go that could hold it. I walked out through the living room to the utility room, got my coat and hat and went outside.

I remember a sunny day, though it was February 3 and there was snow on the ground. Outside I had no better idea where I could park my body but at least I had escaped the house. I found my best friend Steve Osborn coming home from school. We exchanged pleasantries. How does one talk about these things? I felt like a liar and a fool. When we got to his house his mother was at the door. "How's your father, Fred?" Parents seemed to have secret modes of communication; they knew everything. I blurted out "My Dad's dead!" and threw myself into her arms and sobbed. "I didn't know!" Steve called out guiltily. Fade to black.

Woulda, shoulda, coulda...they're part of my inheritance and, likely, part of everyone who has lost someone dear. All the things unsaid and undone come rushing to the fore, along with all things said and done that provide the fuel for endless revisiting, searching for previously unseen keys in all prior encounters to unlock the codes of death. Death is mysterious enough when not hidden from view. Once hidden, left undiscussed and unaddressed, it becomes a black hole, sucking all subsequent speculation into perpetual darkness.

I learned this lesson well from losing my father, even more so because my feelings about him were so ambivalent. After his death, I would lie in bed at night ruminating on all our encounters, especially the most recent. Was it the last time he beat me that I told him I wished he were dead? Was it some previous time? Did he really respond by saying "Someday you may get your wish," or did I just imagine it? When he beat me with his belt did I often say, "I hate you!" or was it only once? Did he really praise the fact that I loved "Peanuts" comics to our family friends? Did he ever once say, "I love you?" I was haunted.

His sudden and permanent exit at the unlikely age of 41 taught me at nine that death is an ever-present possibility. We never know where or when it might strike. Unlike lightning, it can be on the sunniest of days. The weather, the place, the circumstances, with others or without, clothed or unclothed, fed or hungry, anxious or at peace, prepared or not, all these conditions are irrelevant. Death will strike. Any second, any minute, any day. In the wake of someone being disappeared, somehow beamed up to another place and time, those of us who remain become, like the aptly named TV series, The Leftovers.

Dad's death also taught me that dying is always available as the final solution. Its dramatic finality is accessible anytime to resolve any problem. It puts all outstanding questions or problems to rest. Whether problems with myself or problems with others, it solves everything. So death became the logical endgame for any situation I found myself in; for any and all problems, large or small, it was the default option: I can always kill my adversary or myself. Even minor conflicts or challenges could be solved through death scenarios. Properly absorbed and contextualized, put in its place, death can be a great teacher and guide, reminding us to remain up to date, always "complete" with as many people and situations as possible. But imaginatively sought as the end zone for every challenge, it becomes debilitating. Death became my great panacea. Cue neurosis.

Still, I couldn't grasp its embodied essence. I couldn't comprehend its finality. How can it be that someone is in your life one day, seemingly forever, and the next day gone forever without a trace? My dad literally vanished. What accounts for this? I would lie in my bed trying to understand. "Forever. And forever and forever. And forever and forever beyond that. And forever and forever beyond *that*." Each time I said "forever" I would pause until I could collect myself. Then, once I felt like I was beginning to grasp it, I would say "forever" again, piling it on, over and over, repeatedly, until I started to get dizzy and I could feel myself floating, becoming weightless, losing my moorings in time, drifting upward into an endless future. It was my first reckoning with infinity. I willed myself to understand it. Without knowing it, I was trying to land an intellectual concept in my body. It scared the shit out of me.

Despite their intensity at the time, I largely forgot those nights of empyrean terror until 50 years later. I was on a Zen retreat reciting the Heart Sutra. Then it hit me. "Gate, gate, para gate, parasam gate, Bodhi swaha." The Les Hixon translation: "Pure awareness is transcending, ever transcending, transcending transcendence, transcending even the transcendence of transcendence. This is Awakened Mind! Swaha!" There it was. My childhood experience suddenly reflected back to me in sacred text. The Infinite described. *Transcending transcendence, transcending even the transcendence of transcendence.* More than simply described, the infinite was pointed toward, with the pathway to realizing it made clear. The text doesn't describe death per se. It describes something beyond death, and something beyond life, something eternal and unversed, boundless and free. In my juvenile way I was reaching for that same expression, beyond dualities of on/off, night/day, in/out, trying to fathom what lies beyond the cycle of birth and death. With the clarity of perfect hindsight, transposing this sublime adult perspective over my real childhood distress was a stunning Aha moment for me. Or as Hollow Bones Zen practitioners say, Swaha!

A similar experience occurred again in my 50s, again while on meditation retreat. Meditating one morning, I realized I'd been a closet meditator since my youth. It started in mid-adolescence, when I was 15 or 16 years old. Nights when I arrived home drunk and stoned, before going to bed I would sit in a lawn chair on our back stoop, staring out at the yard, peering into the darkness. I was aware of the extremely loud ringing in my ears. I created a game for myself that I loved to play. I'd listen for the sounds of the night, to see if I could hear them above that infernal inner ringing.

There wasn't much to hear. The little neighborhood in our small town of Champaign, Illinois was pretty quiet. There might be a squirrel. An occasional breeze to make the oak leaves rustle, to make the pine needles sway. What I most wanted, I believe, was to come back into stillness, into clarity. I wanted to find myself again after being away—lost in a wash of substances, hiding in personas to make myself liked, drifting in fears unconsciously felt, unacknowledged. But even if I could have articulated it I don't think it was "myself" I was looking to return to. I didn't like myself enough to seek that. It was the "not me" I was seeking, my *non*-self. Just clarity. Resting in awareness. Being alert and comfortable with what is. After pausing for a half hour or more I would go to bed. Even if my ears were still ringing, I always felt renewed and calm.

Though it took me 35 more years to recognize it, I had taught myself meditation.

Though I partied much less as I got older, I irregularly recommenced an unconscious yearning for meditation. In 1991, when I was 36, Pam Marks, Chuck Olin and I were finishing *Out of the Silence* at Chuck's studio in Chicago. It had taken us a long time to find the proper form for the story, and the year of final editing had taken its toll on all of us. Pam asked me one day what I'd like to do when we were finished. The first thing that came to mind was an image of the statues on Easter Island. I said I'd like to sit beside one of those statues, facing East, to look out over the ocean "To see what comes. No matter how long it takes."

What I yearned to say but didn't yet have the skill to recognize was that I actually wanted to *be* one of those statues. To sit—back straight, eyes open—unmoved, not swayed by anyone's needs, not needing anything myself, present, and alert to all. To sit there like a statue—timeless and awake. To touch and re-touch the eternal.

How and why it took me so long to get my ass to the cushion to officially learn meditation is inexplicable, yet somehow also the story of my life. When I finally found my way to my first meditation retreat in 1995 I was terrified. I couldn't imagine a worse fate than four days of silence alone with my own mind. Those were the days of *Hoop Dreams'* phenomenal ride, my breakout film, and I was still enraged at my partners. Did I connect any of these formative stories, any of my previous aspirations toward so-called mindfulness, with this event? Not a chance. But I was wholly aware of my fears: "I can't talk for four days! Are you kidding me?!" I assumed I'd spend my time as I often did—revisiting wounds, fantasizing revenge, swimming in the pools of fury. Then, to top it off, I imagined thinking, "I'm paying money for this?!"

Instead, to my amazement and everlasting gratitude, I experienced four days of increasing calm and clarity. I discovered that if I just stayed present to what was actually happening here and now in my life that it was invariably better than anything that was going on in my mind. I find insufficient the expression "my mind is a runaway train." *My* mind is a hijacked jet piloted by a suicide bomber. Thank god I found meditation. I don't care that it took me 40 years to realize I'd been unconsciously reaching for Buddhist teachings since I was a child. Though the cliché, "Better late than never," holds much truth for me, so does the little known quote from Mark Twain: "I've lived through some terrible things in my life, some of which actually happened."

When I was nine I was too possessed by shock to be obsessed with fear and loathing. On the way to my Dad's funeral, I walked to the car with my Dad's younger brother—the man who at ten was led by my 15 year old father out of the rioting city of Frankfurt after Kristallnacht to the care of Dutch refugee officials, who spent those next 12 months as the war began with a Dutch farm family, only to be fetched by their half-dead father who somehow managed to escape Buchenwald to claim his boys and spirit them across the Atlantic on one of the last ocean liners to make the voyage to NYC in January, 1940. My uncle put his hand on my bony shoulder and said, "Well Freddy, you're the man of the house now."

Nowadays we laugh at the inappropriateness of such statements. Maybe in the back of his mind he was thinking about what he would have done if my father hadn't been there to save his life. But his words didn't seem inappropriate to me. I wanted to be that man, to care for my mother, older sister and younger brother. I wanted to live up to that responsibility. I thought my father's death and my uncle's recognition somehow combined to anoint me a man. It would be many years before I understood the conceit of that. I was no more a man than my sister or brother or mother. But that moment planted a seed in me, one that would continue germinating throughout my lifetime. How to become that man of integrity and honor I yearned to be? How to hold responsibility for the wellbeing of those I love?

My mother thought it unwise for us children to attend my Dad's burial. But we did attend the funeral. I remember counting the bricks behind the altar as a way to focus my mind. Most likely it was accomplishing something like the opposite, diverting me from my feelings. I couldn't really comprehend what was happening. How could I suddenly be at my father's funeral? The man who was walking and talking with me a few days before, the pillar of my family, my Dad, the Earth to my Moon? How could I be going to 4TH grade, a kid like all the other kids, then suddenly be different, separated, told it's not OK to participate in recess with all the other kids when that's in fact what I wanted very much to do? I remember my sister sobbing through much of the ceremony. I couldn't yet experience the emotional dimensions of this new reality. I was in shock. Most of the adults around me were probably also in shock. He was so vital, seemingly in great health, suddenly gone at 41.

Someone whisked the three of us kids home rather than to the cemetery for the burial. Just as both my parents thought it inadvisable to share the truth with us about their political past (they had been Communists and my Dad was called before the House UnAmerican Activities Committee and subsequently blacklisted), my mother thought it wise not to have us witness the last rites. Admirably well-meaning choice; big mistake. Just as we grew up sensing that there was a secret to our parents' history that explained much of their behavior, my siblings and I subsequently suppressed much of the emotional reality of Dad's death. It's a system I've never seen succeed. Parents who think they're doing their best to "protect" their children from harsh truths only succeed in driving the unnamed pain deeper. What isn't faced and addressed directly surfaces later in sideways, dysfunctional behaviors.

While secretly obsessing over it, I grew up officially disregarding death, shrugging it off as "no biggie," never grieving, thoroughly ignorant to how the repressed grief, anger, and fear would drive much of my behavior until the source issues were finally met. Noteworthy examples: the sudden abandonment by a girlfriend when tears spilled out of me in a torrent during my 32ND year; the betrayal by a business partner when rage devoured my pancreas, contributing to me becoming an insulin-dependent diabetic in my 42ND year; the terror and obsession with dying shading my entire life until the death of Tracy in my 60TH year.

All of these losses opened abandoned mines, all leading to the same underground chamber of my father's death. A wound like that doesn't go away. It lodges underground until surface drilling coaxes it to life again.

There followed many years in which my dad's name was never spoken in our house. I drove all my questions and fears inside and never once had a conversation with my siblings or mother about my dad. Though the term didn't exist for another 15 years, I basically grew up with post-traumatic stress. With my peers, whenever they asked about him, I simply said he was dead. That ended the conversation. They never inquired further. When other friends' fathers died it always seemed an element of high drama—one was a Captain who died in a plane crash, another hung himself in the family garage after being pursued by police for embezzling bank money. Their deaths were elements in action/adventure stories. There was plot to follow and narrative to provide closure, even if some wore the black hat of the bad guy. My Dad was a good guy, he wore the white hat, yet his death seemed like inexplicable happenstance.

I unconsciously searched for ways to understand it. Judeo-Christian practices, which I never studied but nonetheless absorbed through the dominant culture, struck me as thoroughly inadequate superstition. So that dynamic of outward silence and internal chatter about death continued for many years. It no doubt contributed to my readings into eastern spirituality in my teens. When I was 14, I picked Alan Watts' *The Book* off my parents' shelf. Five years later I read Ram Dass's *Be Here Now*. Those guides, and other books about Eastern philosophy, provided productive means for me to think about all the big questions, including my father's death.

On the 16TH anniversary of his death in 1981, on the advice of her therapist, my mother decided to finally assemble the family at my father's gravesite. It was my first time there. We stood in the deep snow in front of his modest stone and observed a simple Jewish service led by a thin, threadbare young Rabbi who seemed to have stepped out of the pages of Dostoevsky. Since I had arrived in town hours earlier wearing only sneakers, my mother graciously bought me my first real pair of winter boots, which served me well for the next 35 years. Afterward, we retired to her therapist's office where we spent the next few hours asking any questions we wanted about his death. It was then that I learned how unintentionally complicit my mother was in his dying. Following his first heart attack at home on the night of February 2nd, she was by his side in the hospital the following morning. "Try Werner, try…" she said, as he lay on the bed monitored by machines. He did. He sat up. Then his heart completely gave out and he fell over, dead.

Hearing this episode did little to reinforce faith in my parents' wisdom. I concluded a number of things. It's stupid to exhort people to exert themselves further when they're already in bodily distress. Better to encourage them to relax, breathe and be at peace. It also confirmed for me the futility of macho behavior. No man is so great a fool as when he ignores his present circumstances through assertion of will. Though my father's tremendous force of will had powered him through the Nazis, through the McCarthy Period, through a new country, language, and culture, through poverty and the Second World War, when faced with the reality of death he finally succumbed to hubris.

But even these revelations never solved the mystery of his dying so young, which the autopsy only deepened. There was suspicion of his having a congenital heart defect but this was never confirmed: the autopsy was inconclusive. Most likely it was Hypertrophic Cardiomyopathy, first discovered in 1958, and certainly not commonly understood or diagnosed in 1965. But the doctor did suspect he was pre-diabetic since he had slightly elevated blood sugar levels. Had my father lived longer he might well have manifested full on Type 1 diabetes. That seemed like a productive explanation since most long-term diabetics die from cardio-vascular disease and eventual heart attack.

I was exactly his age at death, 41, when first diagnosed with diabetes. That year was a huge psychological hurdle for me, as I'd spent a good number of months preceding that birthday with low-level dread. "Maybe it's my turn to die," I thought. Having survived that year with tremendous relief, it was only decades later that I made the age connection between the onset of my diabetes and his. Maybe I didn't get away so cleanly after all.

We had other significant commonalities that emerged too. Six years after that belated funeral ceremony, in another session with my Mom and her therapist, I reflected on how lucky I was that Dad had died before the wild years of my teens. In keeping with the fashion of the day I grew my hair long and wore ripped jeans and beads. I always assumed my father would've hated that look. Instead, my mother startled me by responding, "Your Dad was a non-conformist. He probably would've been fine with all that."

Certainly the voice of my internal critic, that sense of never being good enough, is his voice, or one patterned after his. He was an educated, brilliant, cultured man. Even within his short life span, he accomplished a lot and seemed capable of anything. Everyone loved him. Roger Ebert revered him and when I met him, he told me my dad was part of why he became a film critic. When my dad died in 1965 Roger wrote a beautiful handwritten note to my Mom expressing his love and admiration.[1] Success and high achievement were what my Dad simply expected. Love was not so easily won. Even today, I still carry his judgments as self-hatred.

Robert Bly, one of the godfathers of "men's work," says American men are the walking wounded, unconsciously seeking their father's blessing. That's a fair summation of my life and most of the men I know. The evidence of that wounding and all that unconscious seeking is too great to recount here, though a great deal of my artistic life has been spent studying the issue. Suffice it to say that too many men are suspended adolescents, ruled by their fears and unconscious appetites, still trying to prove something to Daddy. Unfortunately, given the immeasurable extent of horrible consequences, those men largely run the world.

I unconsciously steered away from strong Type A males through my teens and 20s. I projected all the worst aspects of my father onto them, thought them arrogant, full of themselves, self-appointed leaders seeking obeisance. I was equally unconsciously drawn to the company of women and gay men. I felt my emotions were safe with them, and I could risk being vulnerable. It was many years, not until 1995, when I started "men's work" and for the first time began to understand how

---

1. See page 18.

even the toughest men are precious and tender if approached in the right way. I learned only then, as a heterosexual man, how to give and get love from other men. My life was never the same. Within a very few years my poles entirely flipped and I found myself more comfortable and trusting of men than women. Then in 2002, I met Tracy. She alone was responsible for helping me redress and re-right the balance, where, hopefully, it remains today, trusting of and open to the hearts of both men and women in equal measure.

When my dad died in 1965 Roger wrote a beautiful handwritten note to my Mom expressing his love and admiration.

> February 5, 1965
>
> Dear Mrs. Marx,
>
> When such a wonderful person as Werner is lost, there is little that can be said but a great deal that is felt by those who knew him and grieve his death. As one of Werner's many, many friends, I want to express my sorrow to you and to your children. There can be no adequate compensation, no simple words which can take away the pain of this unexpected tragedy. There can only be the knowledge that Werner led a full and useful life, loved by his friends, a devoted husband and wise father. The depth of his enthusiasm, the quickness of his wit, his willingness to take part in all those projects which students enlisted his aid for — all of these uniquely human qualities cannot be forgotten, and they resulted in the creation of a good, a full, a creative life. Please accept my most personal sympathy in this time of grief and in the difficult days ahead.
>
> Sincerely,
> Roger Ebert

CHAPTER 2

MIRIAM MARX
NOV. 3, 1926—MARCH 7, 2013

ONE OF THE greatest gifts my mother ever gave me was a peaceful and timely death. Her painless and rapid passing was a blessing for all of us siblings—modeling a happy transition, in gratitude for the fullness of her life, at peace with everything. I was holding her hand and looking into her eyes as she died. I'm not sure anyone else cared to share that final moment with her but it meant a lot to me. My brother and sister were present at her bedside, as was Tracy and my brother's wife. But they were chatting and missed her final breaths.

The grandchildren had been brought in before to say their goodbyes, and unlike the way dying is so often mishandled for young kids, I feel that this was exactly as it should be. My sister's daughter was too spooked and refused. But my brother's two daughters, aged 10 and 12, held her hand and said, "I love you grandma." Simple, dignified, meaningful. Exactly the opportunity I wished I'd had with my father. Largely in keeping with the way my mother lived her life.

With the soul of an artist who always treasured learning, my Mom played a number of significant roles during her 87 years: published poet, ministerial candidate, political activist, scholar, feminist and women's community builder…a lover of song, art, and life in all its forms. She left us a typically dignified and loving letter when she died, that we found with her will.[2]

Born in 1926, the child of immigrant garment workers, and raised during the Depression, she often went hungry in her youth. She went to work fulltime immediately following high school and never managed to earn a professional class income her entire life. She lived quite frugally, holding the clear intention to leave this life with some money for her children. Near the end, given how rapidly medical expenses unreimbursed by insurance companies diminished her savings, it was the speed of her demise that made the miracle of a small inheritance possible, managing to leave me, my brother, and my sister about $25k each. For her this was an enormous accomplishment. As much as it can be said that someone chooses the timing of her death, that marvel was consistent with her longstanding intention.

She married my father in 1945. Though he was a literal refugee, in a very real sense they were both refugees. Despite being born in this country, my Mom might well have been born in Russia, which her parents left to escape pogroms. Her native language was Yiddish and she grew up surrounded by other poor Jewish immigrants in the Strawberry Mansion neighborhood of Philadelphia, PA.

No one bothered to mention to her as she went off to school that first time in 1931 that she would be encountering a new language—English. Maybe the adults in her world themselves didn't know. She spent much of her first year in school in a state of shock, learning a foreign language from scratch. Bewilderment and confusion were her childhood companions, compounded by the fact that her father abandoned the family when she was two and her much older brother left around the same time. Miriam was left alone with her moth-

---

2. See pages 37 and 38.

er—undiagnosed, but likely schizophrenic. Effectively homeless, she had to raise herself to adulthood.

Mom arrived in Champaign-Urbana, IL in 1959 when my Dad took a job at the University of Illinois as a Professor of German. Like her husband, she had a sharp mind. Unfortunately, she didn't have the flexibility and range he possessed. Though deep, her mind tended to run along well-traveled routes. I put myself in that same category. Only one of many similarities we share.

Fulfilling my Dad's intentions prior to his death and her own wishes, she took us all to Freiburg, Germany for a year of study and travel in 1970-1971. That was my first introduction to the wonders of Europe and she made it grand, not only taking us through Germany, but repeatedly to the UK, France, and Switzerland, and on separate trips to the Netherlands, Italy, Austria, Czechoslovakia, and Hungary.

Unfortunately, that was my 15TH year and I had a bad case of teenage rebellion. My mother had the good sense to give me my own room in our tiny three room apartment. She shared a bed with my sister and made my ten year old brother sleep on the living room couch. But I desperately needed to break away from her and I didn't know how. I made her life miserable. Until the day she died, despite our subsequent rapprochement and years of great relations, my mother always referred to that as the time I was possessed by demons.

Once I was married, every time my mother made that comment Tracy would laugh and shake her head. It's no accident that my *Boys to Men?* series focuses on 15 year old boys and my teen *Rites of Passage* work similarly highlights the challenges of that age. Unfortunately, I don't think my mother ever drew the connection, certainly never enough to recast that time in Germany into a new light. I myself wasn't savvy enough to notice the connection until years later.

During the summer following my junior year of high school, when I was 16, I moved into a large house with a group of friends, inhabiting all five bedrooms by way of communal living. This was our summer of love, 1972. We watched in wonder as George McGovern won the Democratic Presidential Nomination. Anything seemed possible. Though I worked with my best friend Matthew as a Day Camp Counselor, we drove to lots of concerts and partied with abandon. Naturally there were plenty of drugs, though we mostly just smoked pot, listened to music, had sex, and ate poorly.

My mother came to regret her decision to allow me to do this. The subsequent school year was hell for her as I refused any further parenting. Once I returned home at 4am from a concert in St. Louis. That might have been the last time she tried to hit me. I was 6'5" by then, pretty strong, and not inclined to take anything from anybody. I took to spending days at my girlfriend's. Mid-year Mom came to the school to try to assert leverage through my counselor and basketball coach. But it was fruitless. My drug and alcohol use notwithstanding, I was Vice-President of the Student Council, Co-Captain of the basketball team, and a fine student with fine grades. It was a huge relief for both of us when I moved out of the house for good following my graduation. The subsequent 4-5 years were a cool period of détente. I remember her dropping off a 19TH birthday gift for me by leaving it inside the door at the bottom of the stairs. She shouted up to my roommate to notify him it was there before hurrying off the porch.

In retrospect, I can see much more clearly how I grew up with some distrust of family systems due to the power struggles I had with my mother and how I felt my brother and sister consistently sided with her against me. Though it's not the only reason, it certainly contributed to me not wanting to marry, to have children, or to live a traditional middle class "two car garage" life.

No doubt, this was also an inherited notion since both my father and mother were exiled from their own respective families for being Communists. We had almost no contact whatsoever with extended family during our childhood. Couple that conditioning with what I now consider to be my own genetic predisposition against doing things the way others do, I'm disinclined to expect safety in family structures.

No wonder I enjoy filming families other than my own, learning the intricacies, what makes them work and not work. *Hoop Dreams* is only the most obvious example. My films *Boys to Men?* and *The Unspoken*, even *Journey from Zanskar* evidence this theme. The greatest single complement I ever received for my work came from Robin Buie, an African-American working class mom in Newark, NJ during the filming of *Boys to Men?* She told me that due to my process of filming her family, my questioning her during interviews about the perspective of her children, she had come to understand her own son better.

It's of course easier to assist others than to aid oneself. It's no accident that I ended up in California while my brother and sister, and eventually my Mom, all lived in New York. I never felt entirely at home in my family. Maybe it goes back to the aftermath of my father's death, trying, and failing, to be a parent to my siblings and a partner to my Mom. It's easy to say, "Well, of course, that's completely dysfunctional. Not succeeding is a good thing." But I wasn't constitutionally suited to playing those roles. Even as an adult, I'm not equipped with the patience and sustaining interest needed to parent. Historically deficient in governing myself with wisdom and discipline, I can be far too lackadaisical. I feel certain that if I had chosen to have a family, at some point I'd most likely let everything go. I'm the rebel. And like most rebels in family systems, I became the black sheep.

That sense of outsider, not fitting in, shadowed me long before my mother and I went to war. My sister, like most eldest siblings, became the surrogate parent. I took her direction even less kindly than my mother's. But my brother also felt like a collaborator with my Mom against me. Three against one. Partly because they live relatively near each other, but largely from long-standing habit, to this day my sister and brother maintain more frequent contact and have a deeper relationship.

My lifestyle is also significantly different. They own homes and have their own families. They are well paid, accomplished professionals, working 9-5 jobs, maintaining all the rudiments of traditional middle class life. Maybe that outsider status that I'm describing is what all artists feel. "Where do I fit in?" is a commonplace artist's question. I've long puzzled over a fundamental paradox of my work—wanting my outsider visions to be embraced by the mainstream. Oddly enough, I believe my family dynamic makes me most like my mother—herself an outcast from her family, living a life apart.

That wound of betrayal, standing alone against greater forces, is a common theme of my life. The few against the many. David vs. Goliath. "Who will side with me?" is a key question I often ask. I experienced it toward the end of making *Hoop Dreams* and at other key moments in my life. But my brother and sister found their ways into mainstream culture in ways that I have not, due again, in no small part to my own insistence on succeeding solely on my own terms. Though we get along fine and resolve disputes far more equitably than most families, the residue of those longstanding hurts has not been conducive to abiding intimacy. I love my brother and sister but a part of me still doesn't trust them. With her own family of origin, I believe my mother lived out her entire life this way. That's the family system that was modeled for me.

Perhaps spiritual pursuits became a substitute. In 1972, she joined the Urbana Unitarian Church. Its offshoot the Red Herring Press published her poetry chapbook *Armor and Ash-*

es in 1982. She moved to Beijing for two years in 1985 after I got her a job as a foreign language instructor. When she returned in 1987 I scheduled a four-hour session with my therapist to once and for all clean out the specters of the past that lay between us. We reviewed the countless battles that culminated with me moving out of the house at 16. That seminal rapprochement, one of the greatest gifts she ever gave me, became the foundation on which we built our largely peaceful subsequent years as aspiring peers.

Ever thirsting for meaning and fulfillment in life, and perhaps that deeper sense of family, in 1991 she began study to become a Unitarian-Universalist Minister, culminating in her graduation in 1997 at the age of 70 with a Masters of Divinity. I attach a typically thoughtful letter she wrote to an acquaintance who was considering traveling the same road.[3]

She was rightfully proud of what she accomplished. But she was never ordained. For reasons not entirely clear the U-U review panel turned her down. Unlike their standard ordination policy that allows every candidate three opportunities for evaluation, they told her, "Don't come back." In keeping with her standard practice of full-on intensity, my guess is she shared too much, too emotionally, too authentically about the challenges of her past, came across as volatile or unstable, and freaked out the panel. She was devastated. That had been her sole aim for six years and, given her age, she had been a star candidate often featured in local newspapers. She went into a three-year depression and never again entered a U-U church. Eventually, she took up with the Quakers. But the Quakers don't ordain. With her degree, she still could have provided pastoral care in hospitals and community agencies but it never appealed to her.

---

3. See pages 39 and 40.

I am so like her — nowhere more certainly than in the devastation following serious disappointment. All four of my last films have been commercial and, to some extent, critical failures. Each successive setback, though easier than the one previous, has shattered me. Perhaps par for the artist's course. I hold myself responsible for not compromising, for not creating more commercially acceptable work. But, despite the challenges the work presents, I also still hold festival programmers, critics, distributors and broadcasters responsible for ignoring it.

My mother taught me about victimization well. Coming of age during the Depression she grew to expect to be mistreated and misunderstood. She adopted a "beg for mercy" posture when dealing with strangers. Pleading poverty, she regularly sought special treatment and favors from home repairmen, lawyers, doctors, and other service professionals. Highly sensitive by nature, she felt easily offended by things others might say or do. She often felt battered by the world, the victim of people and forces impossible to affect. She never responded to life's constant call to learn conflict resolution. Fortunately, I've learned many effective forms of conflict resolution. But I'm constructed from the same psychological cloth.

Wherever there's a victim there's also a perpetrator. The two go hand in hand. My mother would perpetrate passive-aggressively, usually by turning her back on her "victimizers." Once and for all. For life. Forever. She lost a lot of friends that way. Perpetration also took the form of the cause of justice. When victimized, she would wrap herself in the flag of righteous indignation and social justice and set out on the warpath of revenge.

I share these traits. My default mode is victim. I can walk out of my house in the morning, have a pigeon shit on my head and, rather than laugh, declaim in anguish, "Why me, Lord?!" My perpetrator also looks like my mother's. I burn friendships by writing people off. Those who betray me usually go down in a hail fire of righteous bullets. At least in my fantasies. It's not enough to reach and find compromises with my tormentors, discovering solutions that work for all, the win-win. I want my victimizers to go down hard, all the way down. I want them dead.

This is important stuff to be aware of. If this dynamic is to stop with me, if I want to break the family chain, I have to constantly work to mitigate against many of my "natural" impulses. It's not easy but I'm making progress. Recurring pain is a great motivator.

Perhaps because of the comparable depths of our regular despair, my mother and I also shared a spiritual yearning. I have practiced Buddhism for almost 30 years. I wanted to understand the cause of my suffering and root it out. In relatively short order I understood how I was causing most of my own anguish. But it took me most of those 30 years before I finally resolved to do something about it. Like her, only late in the game did I pursue ordainment. Just in time. My intensified practice became part of the support structure to move me through Tracy's dying and all my subsequent grief.

I think my mother lied about her age and married at 17. She wed my father in the Philadelphia courthouse. In dramatic contrast, it took me until I was 47 before I was finally ready for marriage. On my wedding day, in a most different setting at Green Gulch farm in Marin County California, my mother exclaimed repeatedly, "This is the happiest day of my life." She was known for hyperbole. Based on 25 years of hard data—my prior relationships with beautiful, eligible women whom I'd never married, she presumed I was beyond redemption. She assumed I'd never make my commitment to my work secondary to anyone. A reasonable assumption since that's what I always told her. Nonetheless, when my brother—married, with two beautiful daughters—heard her say that, he looked at her with a "What am I? Chopped liver?" expression. My sister—also married, also with her own beautiful daughter—took it in stride. Without question, the day I married Tracy was the happiest day of *my* life.

Being writer/directors, Tracy and I gave a lot of thought to designing the ceremony and to our wedding vows.[4] In typical wedding vows you don't usually find "I vow to go toe-to-toe with your shadow to help you recognize, accept, and love your own darkness." That one was my idea, though word crafted and shifted toward the positive by Tracy. I can go through each vow and confidently point out who was most responsible for writing it. I'm proud of them all, even more proud to say that they were largely observed. The biggest challenge for me was Tracy's: "I vow to embrace your family as my own." At my worst, I'm a hypocrite who wants to save the human race but can't stand human beings. I often have little patience for individual human foibles and I don't suffer fools gladly. It's taken me years to come to terms with my own family and our various dysfunctions. I feared and to some degree failed at embracing Tracy's family, complete with their own dysfunctions.

Over time however, I started to view Tracy and me combined as family. It started when I was challenged to do so by a brother from the ManKind Project (MKP). "What do you mean you don't have a family? What about Tracy?" I confessed to him that I hadn't thought of her, of us, in that way. A family had kids, I thought. Otherwise, you were just a couple. I thought you needed at least three people to make a family.

Once my dad died, we were four in my family of origin. But that was a shaky four. My mother carried suicidal tendencies and eventually bequeathed them to me. She hinted often at taking her life. She occasionally began sentences with "If I weren't around…" or "After I'm gone…" Her despair is not

---

4. See page 41.

surprising, given the challenges she faced raising three kids on life insurance money, social security, and an assistant's salary. Once, my sister made my mother's implicit emotional blackmail wholly explicit to my brother and me when she told us our mother would kill herself if we didn't behave. I was probably 12, my brother 7, my sister 14. Unfortunately for all of them, her admonition failed to constrain my behavior.

Mom was lonely and, though she had boyfriends over the years, she never married again after my dad died. Prior to her crushing disappointment with the U-U Church, she gave up on her dream of becoming a college professor. The eight years it took her to get her BA and the three it took her to get her Master's had exhausted her. I think her lack of self-confidence caught up with her too. She defaulted to her working class roots and took jobs, often secretarial, that were beneath her skill set.

It was the summer of 1983 when, gathered at my sister's apartment in Brooklyn to visit friends and her aging father, she called the four of us together in the tiny living room and asked us for permission to kill herself. I was 27 at the time, my sister 30 and my brother 23. She began with a preamble about repressing her pain when my Dad died in order to keep us alive, "like a mother bear fighting for her cubs." "I was crazy in those years." No doubt with PTS. She went on to recount her many subsequent years of struggling with depression.

My sister was incensed and said she felt violated by the asking. I was more empathetic; I understood where she was coming from. Were she to take her own life she didn't want to leave us shocked and heart-stricken. Still, I said it was not suitable for us to grant permission, much less to do what I think she really wanted and bestow a blessing on her plans. It was really just a cry for help. She wanted her despair known. We were all frustrated and at a loss, ill equipped to deal with the situation, much less to articulate remedies. I believe it was my sister who encouraged her to seek therapy.

Though Tracy was far more able at articulating her feelings than my mother, she was similarly not easy to assist. Fiercely independent, and because she was perfectly capable in so many areas of her life, Tracy was a difficult person to aid. She had a do-it-all-yourself shadow. There was a period of time about three years before she died when, on the advice of my friend and mentor Fugen Tom Pitner, every day I asked her what particular service I could do for her that day. It was a perfect challenge for each of us. I can be self-involved and tend to forget serving my partner. Given her acute self-reliance, she was forced by this interaction to face her own shadow as well. She had a difficult time coming up with anything. Most often it was "make me dinner." Sometimes it was "clean the bathroom for our coming guests" or "take out the garbage." After a while expressing even these small desires seemed burdensome. "Let me think about it," she'd say, then never get back to me. She stopped giving me answers and I stopped asking. She grew bored. The requests seemed tiresome. They would cease, the service issues unaddressed, until the next hurts would surface. She'd default to doing everything herself until one day she'd get tired of it and ask me again to start doing things for her.

We usually spoke our deepest truths to each other and did our best to state clearly and directly what we wanted. She wasn't keen that she had to ask, and she got mad about it numerous times, since, after all, "I should just *know*," but eventually she learned to ask me for hugs. Like everyone, she had expectations of what "normal" people do in a marriage. That included hugging and holding her with great frequency. I was neither raised that way nor inclined by instinct to do that. However, I usually respond readily and happily to clearly stated requests to fill in blind spots.

She stood ready to provide the same for me. When I'm on my game, I too can ask clearly for what I need. After being slimed on by one person or another I would come to her and say, "Tell me please the man you see before you. Because I don't think I'm a man deserving of the abuse I just took." She would share some positive and truthful observations, usually some variation of "You're a good man," and then hug me. I believe having the awareness and the facility to ask for this kind of support is a huge mark of relationship success.

That's what made the end of Tracy's life especially poignant and fulfilling for me...I finally got to take care of her. I got to drive her to all her doctor's appointments and accompany her to chemo. I got to bring breakfast to her in bed. I got to run errands for and sometimes with her. I got to fetch her meds and special foods. I got to take her on special outings. I got to give her massages. But only at the very end did she let me clean up her messes.

Back in the early phase of our marriage, after learning to consider the two of us as a complete unit, I had begun to relish the concept of family, of making family with Tracy, of *being* family with her. I hoped to become the primary family breadwinner. I wanted to have Tracy as a "kept woman," to let her retire from teaching and dedicate herself to writing, gardening, and grandchildren. This notion added an additional layer of care and concern to my affections for her. We weren't blood ties but we were *family*. To most people, it probably sounds stupid since it's such a given. But for me it became a revelation. She was my family of choice.

In this way, she healed something in me. I never thought family could mean this level of support, of trust. That dependence could have positive connotations and impact. That intimacy could be this deep and abiding.

At a couple's workshop in 2007, Tracy and I added to our marriage vows by co-creating a family mission statement: "We vow to use creativity in all its forms to live truthfully, compassionately, sustainably, and joyfully in all our relations." I'm as proud of that statement today as when we wrote it. More proud of the fact that we did a fine job living up to it. Right up to and including Tracy's Life Honoring Celebration.

The whole idea of a Life Honoring Celebration was first modeled for me in a ceremony for my friend Marty Feldman. I met Marty during my ManKind Project (MKP) weekend October 1995 in Chicago. We joined the same men's support group and used to meet often at his recording studio in a warehouse on the near north side. In one of our first meetings Marty told us about his cancer. He was dying, maybe not immanently, but nonetheless. "You guys are going to be the ones to bury me," he said. He knew he'd never live to see his young son become an adult.

Nine years later as his days grew numbered, he had his 11 year old boy by his side. Marty sat at the front of the large meeting room in Chicago's MKP Lodge, his wife on his other side. There were almost 100 people there, and others—some, famous musicians that Marty had worked with—were connected by phone throughout the day. I was lucky because I'd received notice two weeks earlier while working on a project in Tehran, allowing me just enough time to wrap up and fly to Chicago with Tracy.

Person after person got up and spoke directly to Marty, sharing funny and often heart-breaking stories and reflections, making it clear how he'd impacted their lives. Three of the eight original men of our support group were there. I cried through much of my speech. But I thanked Marty for many things, including how he often saw through the bullshit I sometimes proffered as wisdom. Except for one notable time which I teased him about. That day, we were ruminating on the phone about death. I told him I fantasized about having everything so neatly resolved and cleaned up at my death that life could close over me like an ocean wave leaving no earthly trace of what I'd done during my lifetime. It was complete bullshit. Romantic nonsense. Somehow that day Marty didn't see through it. Perhaps because he had more important things to be concerned about, like his own real demise, not some fantasy death. That ceremony gave me a new, side mission in life, and I promote these Celebrations wherever I go.

On her 80TH birthday we did something similar for my Mom, though not in a large public space. Her immediate family and a few friends met in one of her favorite restaurants. My brother designed and presented her with a framed photomontage of her entire life. We took turns honoring her, reminding her of various episodes from her life, and each said something of what we treasured about her. I consider it one of the great achievements of her life that she was able to endure. She never killed herself.

We did a more formal Life Honoring Ceremony for Tracy. Hers took place 12 days before she died. It was not easy to get her to agree to do it. A very private and humble person, she had a difficult time picturing the ceremony as anything more than ego inflation. I did my best to convince her that it was really about soul. It was a way for people to reflect back to her how they had seen into her soul and been nourished by it, giving them a chance to honor her before she passed. I broached the subject many times throughout our years together and returned to it repeatedly during her final months. Each time I failed to get her to say yes.

What finally convinced her were two unrelated but interconnected events. Once she went off chemo, Tracy was typically thoughtful in letting a small circle of family, friends, and co-workers know of her impending death. About six weeks before she died, she received a card from one of her colleagues. That colleague expressed in eloquent, impassioned terms what a difference Tracy had made in her life, how Tracy helped her become a better writer, teacher, and person. Tracy was dumbfounded. She had no idea she had impacted this woman in those ways. That card arrived during her sister Shannon's visit. In the course of their conversation about it, Tracy began to ruminate on how many other people might similarly have been impacted by her to a completely unknown degree. I happened into the conversation about that time. That made Tracy mention to Shannon how I'd tried for some time to convince her to allow me to create a Life Honoring Celebration for her. Shannon thought it a wonderful idea and immediately pressed Tracy to accept. So Tracy finally said yes.

We instantly set to work on a date. Within an hour I drafted an invitation. Tracy of course tweaked the writing and improved it. I remember two small but characteristic changes: she thought it best to add, "she will be present" to make it clear she was not dead yet. She also insisted that we recommend that people arrive by public transportation.

> *You're invited to a celebration to honor the life of Tracy Seeley. She will be present. For those of you unfamiliar with her situation please click here: https://www.caringbridge.org/visit/tracyseeley. Details on the event are below.*
>
> The purpose of this celebration is to let Tracy know how she's made a difference in your life and in the lives of others you may know. This sharing allows us to underscore how we are all connected, each a part of the other, and to celebrate that interconnection. Being together in this way also underscores with simplicity and ease how when we gather to speak our heart's truth and are witnessed by others, we deepen our understanding of the very meaning of life and invite grace into our lives.
>
> Ideally, every human being would have this opportunity before they die. Every human being deserves it. In our culture, though,

fear and repression too often deny us this chance. So come prepared to speak your heart's truth; step confidently into the simple reality of a loved one's passing. Use this process to begin your grieving process if that serves you, but also please come prepared too for a lot of laughter and light. This will not be a religious ceremony. All beliefs and non-beliefs are welcome.

Following the sharing of words we will share the blessing of food. Please bring a potluck item…Please, no gifts. Your presence is your gift to us.

None of us can insist on the appearance of grace in this lifetime, but if we create ceremony with great intention and mindfulness we can sometimes set the ground for grace to arrive and bless us all.

Ubuntu,
Frederick Marx
(Tracy's husband)
Date: June 25, 2016

What followed was one of the most wondrous scenes I've been privileged to ever participate in.

I wheeled Tracy in by wheelchair. We sat together at the apex of a horseshoe with our 30 guests radiating in semicircular rows facing us. I welcomed everyone and made a long introduction, presenting our two facilitators, updating everyone on Tracy's health, explaining why we were filming it, and why we were holding the ceremony then. I ended it with a quote and these observations: "'A friend is someone who knows the song in your heart and can sing it back to you when you have forgotten the words.' I forget, question and doubt my life song all the time. But this day is about Tracy. She's much better at it but even she forgets on occasion. So that's your job here today—to sing her life song back to her so she can remember the words. With authenticity and emotional vulnerability. Like our lives, like our deaths…please rest easy in the comfort of knowing that whatever arises is what's meant to be here."

What arose were two hours of heartfelt delight. Tracy was alert, quippy, and beaming love…that is to say, she was her normal self. It still gladdens my heart that we were able to do this for her before she died. No one should leave this planet with anything less.

I'd like to start a worldwide movement to implement practices of culturally appropriate Life Honoring Celebrations. Not to replace funerals but to augment them. Personally, I think it's impractical at best and pointless at worst to sing somebody's praises when they're dead. Perhaps saying lovely things about them at funerals helps us mourn. Saying the same things to them while alive may give us a jumpstart on that mourning. But why not use their dying as an opportunity to grow *ourselves*, to bring us into closer proximity with the reality of death, to face our fears and step willfully into our deepest hearts to speak the truth of what someone means to us? Why not tell them when they're alive? Why not let them see some of the difference they made in the world around them? Even the most troubled and maligned person usually has positively impacted somebody. No matter how difficult anyone's life has been they usually create some ripples of positive change. And I believe that every person longs to know that. We long to *see* it. To know that our existence does *not* all come to naught in the end. That efforts large and small have impacts seen and unseen. It serves each of us to have tangible proof of this before we pass. Life Honoring Celebrations should be every human's birthright. Thank goodness Tracy got to receive hers. Just in time.

To my children:
Don't mourn for me. I have lived a very full life and that is all that one can really ask. I have been very happy I have been very sad My dear husband, my dear children, my dear friends filled the emptiness that was my childhood.

Sholem Alachem asked his children to remember him with laughter. I ask you to remember me with happiness, the happiness of very simple things — a warm sunshiny day with a blue sky — the beauty of growing flowers.

If the tree dies which I had planted over Daddy's grave when I am buried, please plant another one like it. Then when the

> blossoms fall, they can fall on both of us.
> 	Love each other, help each other, for his sake and mine.
> 		Mother.

1045 Woolman Drive
Richmond, IN 47374

March 4, 1996

Thomas Guback
608 W. Michigan
Urbana, IL 61801

Dear Thomas,

    Frederick had told me that you might be writing, and I remembered that when your letter came. I quite understand your hesitations and feelings. How true it is, and how often I have heard it from others: "The more I push it out of my mind, the stronger it comes back." Just so. Your experience parallels my own; let me share that with you.

    The thought of studying for the ministry developed slowly in my mind over a period of time. Finally, I went to talk to my minister. In several ways, some more, some less subtle, he told me I was too old. I accepted his judgment and [tried to] put it out of my mind.

    When a young/middle-aged woman came to serve our church as an intern for six months, I sought her out to talk with her generally about the church, and I spoke of activities I had been involved in. After meeting several times, one day she asked me, Miriam, have you ever thought of going into the ministry? I said yes I had thought of, but I had rejected it because of my age. She said, Nonsense! and my life was changed.

    We seem to need someone who believes in us in order to allow ourselves to listen to, believe in, and respond to God's calling. During my first semester here, in a course called Spiritual Preparation, I discovered we had all come only very reluctantly and dragging our heels. It seemed God was not only leading us but perhaps even pushing us from behind. Maybe that's how it has to be, for us to disbelieve and then feel a humility that it is ministry that we are called to.

    I think those of us who come to ministry late in life have much to offer people we will serve. Our life experience of coping with family situations, careers, disappointments and setbacks has widened and deepened our understanding of life, its trials and its joys.

You too were less than encouraged by your priest in Champaign. You too were encouraged by another. Listen to him. Be encouraged; get all the help and affirmation you can get from other people. You will need it all. It is a difficult path to choose. Most of all, listen to and believe in the "still, small voice" that speaks to you. I hope the discernment conference at Seabury-Western was also helpful.

The church needs those of us who are radical, who believe in economic justice and the social gospel to make religion relevant to ordinary people and therefore allow us all to be ruled by the law of love and to play out the roles we are meant to play, of peacemakers in this world.

Good Luck!

Miriam

Tracy and Frederick Wedding Vows

August 15, 2003

I commit myself to regular meditation and spiritual training in order to support my own growth and our life together.

I do not depend on you for my growth and care; I vow to take responsibility for my own well-being.

I vow to communicate with honesty and vulnerability; I take responsibility for my own feelings, and for my own actions and reactions.

I vow to clean up anything in myself that hinders a loving relationship with you.

I vow to acknowledge and release my fears of intimacy so that I can fully surrender into union.

I vow to go toe-to-toe with your shadow to help you recognize, accept, and love your own darkness.

I vow to spend time every day being fully present with you.

I vow to show you my appreciation and love in both words and deeds.

I vow to create a tranquil home where fun, play, and creativity are priorities in our life together.

I vow to do my best to make you laugh at least once a day.

I vow to help you reach your fullest potential, maximize your gifts and offer them confidently to the world.

I vow to embrace your family as my own.

I vow to resolve conflict peacefully and with a generous heart.

I vow to enact the enlightened practices in our relationship that I seek in the world.

CHAPTER 3
TRACY SEELEY
APRIL 6, 1957—JULY 7, 2016

When I first met Tracy Seeley I couldn't look into her eyes. They were so beautiful I felt like I couldn't look into them without falling. I was embarrassed. They made me feel exposed, naked, like I was staring at something illicit. So I looked away. Nervously.

On about our 4TH date I stopped her suddenly on the street. "You're not neurotic at all are you?" I don't remember her reaction now but I imagine she laughed slightly. Freud invented psychoanalysis for people like me, people with my background. Educated European Jews. I was a bit stunned to meet someone who didn't fit the patterns of neurosis that I seemed to find in pretty much every other person I encountered. "Well, this is refreshing!"

As I later learned Tracy of course had her own issues, the most notable being that she could be very controlling. Everyone has her or his shadows; there is no escaping that. In recognizing hers I guess you could say I graduated from Freud to Jung. She once told me, without irony, that if I just did what she said I wouldn't be so miserable.

If there were one phrase Tracy used repeatedly that could sum up her character it would be "you're not the boss of me." That's what I heard often when I tried to suggest to her an alternative way of doing something. If she felt even slightly that I was trying to "be the boss," her reaction was swift and merciless. Not coincidentally, this is exactly how I'd also get triggered by her. I can't stand bossiness. Tracy most drove me crazy when she assumed the air of an exasperated teacher dealing with a misbehaving pupil. It felt so condescending. Of course I always felt more justified in pointing out her bossiness than I ever felt about her doing the same to me. Nonetheless, over time, "You're not the boss of me," became a semi-comic tagline that she would say when she felt reactive about something I said or did. Thank god for progress. Hearing her say that and then smiling was like being kissed rather than spanked.

Tracy knew who she was to her deepest core—a mother and an English professor. She didn't moan or fret about what she was on the planet to do. She just did it, every day, with confidence and the complete congruence that comes with self-knowing. Founding the University of San Francisco's "Writing Warriors" was a logical outgrowth of her own disciplined need to set aside time to write. Founding USF's Center for Teaching Excellence was an organic offshoot of her own commitment to be the best teacher to her students she could possibly be. It was a joy to see her discover yet another talent. To complement her superb academic writing, she learned she was a brilliant creative writer. If you haven't yet read her memoir/essay *My Ruby Slippers* run and get it now. You can come to know Tracy the best way possible—through her art. It's what I'm doing again, reading it now to keep her close.

She was the single most mature human being I've ever met. Her acceptance of all life's misfortunes was deep. Perhaps it dated back to her initial diagnosis of cancer in 2002, when she was only 44.... But I suspect it went further. On days when I wanted to put my fist through walls, defeated by my absolute impotence to help her, days when she would puke five times trying to keep food down that first chemo and later opiates would not allow her, she would emerge from the bathroom with a slight smile on her face—genuine—and say, "Dying is really hard for a control freak."

Her delight in the simplest things amazed me. I'm a closet drama queen. She was the opposite -- no recovering narcissist needing spotlights to bask in and chandeliers above crystal pools to find her reflection in. In her final months, no doubt partly to grope back to full consciousness and repossess the vast intelligence which was her birthright—reclaiming it from the chemo and the drugs—she spent hours watching cute kid and animal videos, the kind where birds bathe in a dog's water bowl. This was Majestic Life too and she laughed and cried and relished it all. We would laugh together and remember Miriam Engelberg, Tracy's close friend from her first cancer support group, (dead at 48, leaving a 10-year-old child), who wrote the absolutely true graphic memoir "Cancer Made Me a Shallower Person."

A deep sense of mortality is what brought us together. When we met, she had recently completed her first year of living with cancer—surgery, radiation, chemo…the whole cocktail. I was neurotically obsessed with the idea of dying from Type I insulin-dependent diabetes since I'd recently failed my last ditch alternative healing approach. Likely one of us would die soon, certainly within ten years, so we knew time was short. Later, we had many good laughs, even after her Stage IV diagnosis in 2006, that the joke was going to be on us, that we'd actually live together well into our 80s and die of old age.

Ever the proper Kansas girl she would always thank me when I complemented her. On her clothes, her beauty, her talent…it didn't matter. Sometimes it felt like a mannered reflex but most of the time I could tell she really meant it. That it was somehow not her due, not a simple recognition of what is, something natural in the course of things, but a fulfillment, like a chord of music that otherwise might leave a melody unresolved. It was an ever-resonant expression of her endless gratitude.

Her natural state was buoyant, often humming or singing around the house. She was never happier than lying in bed with a good book. Her capacity for joy and meaning found in reading was boundless. I fall asleep within 4 or 5 pages. She could literally read all day. She rightly sensed I had little to no experience with people like her. *Quiet: The Power of Introverts in a World That Can't Stop Talking* suddenly appeared in our house. When she finished the book she threw it on the bed near me and said, "Read this." That's what an impassioned cry from an introvert looks like. It helped. At least I stopped wondering if she was somehow hiding from the world, retreating behind vast readings. We always aimed to simplify our lives, opting for quiet and unbusyness. Partly, we just got older. But most days my ambivert found happy tranquility with her introvert.

One of my great sadnesses of her last few months was seeing her in bed *not* reading. That more than anything told me the end was near. I took to reading to her. A friend gave her *Dwellings* by Linda Hogan—a book seemingly designed to read to the dying. It was quite the scene. I had to stop reading due to the tears that kept choking me, every sentence a hymn to all that is noble and true on this fragile, precious planet. Tracy drifted in and out of consciousness while listening. What she heard she told me she loved. If ever there were a book perfectly fashioned to intermingle with dream-states, this is it.

In those last months I would rake the coals of my brain to think 'What can I do now to make her life richer, more meaningful?' I thought, Beethoven symphonies? Pre-Raphaelite paintings? Rumi's poetry? Only in her last days did I finally relax and remember she's always been unpretentious, treasuring what's simplest and right in front of her. Still, I could have at least pulled out our wedding photos and revisited that glorious day once more with her.

She surprised me about a month before dying by expressing some career regrets. She certainly had hoped to finish another work of creative non-fiction, based on her extended family's history and their intersection with seminal world events—the WWI U.S. flu pandemic which affected 28% of the U.S. population and killed her grandfather, and the Irish potato famine which brought many of her ancestors to North America. But the truth was that she was too devoted to living life, to savoring all its fullness to be bothered with career achievements.

She acquired new skills simply for the delight she found in learning them. She bought a guitar and taught herself to play quite well. She bought a piano and resurrected smiles in playing not experienced since adolescence. She had long mastered all the "domestic arts," only giving up things like cooking when she lost interest. When she fixed cellphones, installed shelves, reupholstered chairs, and rewired lamps I told her how glad I was that there was a man around the house. Her greatest joy in her last months was sewing a quilt for her as yet unborn grandson. When she realized she couldn't finish the quilt herself she took it to a local store. After they told her the date they expected to finish she told them she would likely be dead by then. These lovely women, so-called strangers, held her while she cried. They finished that quilt in short order and proudly delivered it to her own living hands. Not wanting to leave a single possession ungifted, Tracy left notes, gifts and cards all over the house so that everything she loved could find its way to someone she loved.

How rare is it these days to meet someone who's not an addict? Work, sex, drugs, alcohol, sleep, food, TV…everybody's got something. Not Tracy. Her soul was grounded deep in Kansas soil. Part of why we moved from San Francisco to Oakland was so she could garden. The house we lived in for three years had a small but sumptuous back yard—flowering bushes, a plum tree...Tracy put in her own vegetable garden and dreamed of having chickens. *Farm City*, the wonderful book by our almost-neighbor Novella Carpenter, inspired her deeply. One day she came skipping into the house shouting, "You won't believe what the tomatoes are doing!"

We were welcomed to Oakland in the traditional fashion. Our house was broken into and multiple possessions were stolen. I still suspect the drug-dealing neighbors across the street. The timing was too perfect. I used to drive Tracy to work at 9:30 every morning and return an hour and a half later following a swim. Voila! Sometime in that brief gap, the back-door window was smashed. Our computers were taken along with cash and my postage stamps. As in most similar circumstances, it's primarily the shock and sense of violation that struck us. By far the most painful loss was Tracy's jewelry box. She had a number of pieces that had been handed down to her by her mother, who herself had received them from her mother. They didn't have extreme monetary value but they were of tremendous sentimental importance for Tracy. She had hoped to pass them to her daughters.

It's sad and symbolic how the loss of necklaces and pendants and rings creates gaps in the bequest of meaning and connection to the next generation. Result? We get more breaks in the chain of generativity. One more thing that binds us to our children and grandchildren and great grandchildren, connecting this generation to the next and the next, beyond, through the mystery of time, is forever lost. This grieves me and constitutes one of the gravest injustices of our age. The conscious creation of links in the human experience of time is broken.

It was around that same time that she almost broke her arm in her office. Scared the shit out of me. She got up from her desk and tripped over a cable and went crashing to the floor. I heard the yelp, the smash, and finally the tears, and came running from my office. She had hurt herself, but the tears were as much about the ridiculousness of it all, her clumsiness and shame. Fortunately, the floor was carpeted and she didn't hit her head on the way down. I cradled her as she sobbed and collected herself. Unlike her, if I did something like that, the self-reproach and self-castigation would not so easily subside.

All of us are graced with this thing called Life. We are blessed to have it, double blessed to know we have it. We are all called in our own ways to fulfill the mandate that life has bestowed upon us—to become the greatest, most complete versions of ourselves possible, and to give those gifts that are uniquely ours as freely and widely as possible. Tracy lived this notion with her students, doing everything she could to awaken them to their own greatness. Cards and letters from them testifying to the seminal life transformations they experienced in her classes, some dating back 20 years, arrived almost every day for the first month following her death.

It's hard to make a case that any one person is somehow endowed with a greater portion of life force but Tracy possibly was. Certainly, once her mother died in her mid-60s from her own cancer, Tracy knew her life would be short. Though our marriage wasn't perfect I did everything I could to pour every ounce of love and devotion into her that was possible. I took to stroking her bald head in her last days when even light pressure on her limbs became painful. On her last night, after giving her meds, I was stroking her head telling her how beautiful she was and how I loved her so. Her last words to me were whispered. "Thank you."

We talked about so many important and meaningful things but I don't recall ever telling her what a gift it was for me to walk her last mile by her side.

—§—

IN 2002, BEFORE I seriously practiced Zen, I considered training at San Francisco's renowned Zen Hospice Center. I researched what it would take to work there and had a long conversation with a staff member. I intuited that doing the work would be healing and fulfilling for me. Since childhood and my Dad's death I wanted to understand and experience death in ways I had been disallowed. Before I ever met Tracy and learned about her cancer, I wanted the opportunity to support the dying. Meeting her and talking with the Center, those two wholly unrelated but thematically similar events, occurred within a half year of each other. It took 15 years before I realized the marvel in that, which arrived only through this writing. Though I chose not to train at Zen Hospice Center because of the rigorous time commitment, the universe saw fit to offer me a different opportunity toward the exact same end by ushering Tracy into my life.

We met some months after that decision not to pursue hospice work. After numerous unfulfilling or disastrous meetings with various women, I had forgotten that I still had my dating profile on Salon.com. I had given up. I probably would've removed it if I'd simply remembered. It took me completely by surprise when Tracy reached out to me. Her friend Ron Biela had recommended Salon to her on a recent trip to Colorado when she began research for the book that became *My Ruby Slippers*. In her typically systematic way she reviewed a number of profiles and prioritized her list of potential contacts. I was #1. Being a 6'5" successful filmmaker certainly caught her eye. But she was struck by what I said about being an emotionally self-reliant man, not needing a woman to take care of me. I don't know if that was a reflection of the relationship she had just ended with P or not. But mature masculinity was a theme she resonated with and later mentioned in her book. She never got to Bachelor #2. I made sure.

I wish I still had the emails we sent to each other in those first days. This was back before Tinder, the prehistoric times of Internet dating when pictures of potential mates were not necessarily provided. Nothing of special interest stood out to me when I read her profile. But based on the few clues from my profile she quickly discovered who I was with a rudimentary internet search. Directly after our first email she not only found my bio and much of my work, she also knew what I looked like. I felt disadvantaged and told her so. Unable to see what she looked like, I related my big concern—that she was a dog—though I doubt I was as rude as to use that word. Of the many women I met through Salon who were not outright loonies most of them were not physically attractive to me. Tracy wrote back to assure me that she was not a dog. Of course being humble, she didn't go on to say that she was drop-dead gorgeous.

Given my often-unhappy experiences making appointments for hour-long lunches or dinners to meet women, I learned to insist upon a maximum ten minute first meeting. I don't believe I got the idea from speed dating, which hadn't existed at that point in time. My policy was born of hard trial. Tracy was somewhat taken aback by that suggestion but she agreed. We met at a café near her place that was one of her favorites. I lived not far from there and biked over. The record of that first date is still there in blue ink in my 2002 datebook: "Saturday, Nov. 23: 10:00 Meet Tracy. Café Flore, Market & Noe."

We later marveled that even though we lived within a mile of each other we likely never would have met given our different social and professional worlds. Additionally, in keeping with my lifelong timidity around women, had I even seen her I never would've approached her.

Our initial meeting lasted only five minutes. She was perched at a corner table where I couldn't immediately find her. I was struck by the fact she was reading an Irishman's book of poetry. I thought, "Who reads poetry for fun?" I was impressed. But it was those crystal, compassionate blue eyes that really caught my attention...

Careful to construct an escape hatch I had set that meeting ten minutes before my Tai Chi class. So I made my planned exit. But I immediately emailed her once I returned home and asked her out. "Em, are you free tonight?...Uh, how about now?" She took great satisfaction in telling me she was busy. In fact, she was leaving town the next day and wouldn't be back for a week. In later years, Tracy always relished telling that part of the story, how she was unavailable. I don't know many guys who like playing hard to get but women certainly seem to enjoy it. So we had our first real date ten days later.

Four months later, I proposed to her. We'd fallen asleep on the California King futon on my studio floor after making love. I woke up from low blood sugar and went to drink a glass of juice. Returning to bed I snuggled in to her and thought, "This is stupid. I can play out the rest of my life pretending I'm the Lone Ranger. Or I can do the smart thing and ask this incredible woman to marry me." So I did. Nestled into her there on my futon I popped the question. She rightly wondered whether my proposal could be taken seriously since I had low blood sugar. "Is this a sign of hypoglycemic dementia?" she chuckled. "Does it even count?" I assured her I absolutely meant it. But the truth is I might never have summoned the nerve had it *not* been for hypoglycemia.

There had been one or two other moments in my life when I felt strongly that I should ask my then partner the very same question. My Chicago girlfriend Susan used to ask *me* every Valentine's Day to marry her. One time I felt an overwhelming urge to say yes, not only because of how much fun it would have been to surprise her, but we were very much in love. For a moment at least, saying Yes seemed the right thing to do. Thank goodness I had the better sense not to. Our lives soon pulled us in completely opposite directions. Being married would have served neither of us well, and of course would have precluded me from ever meeting Tracy. Proposing to Tracy might've been the smartest thing I ever did. Diabetes-induced low blood sugar episodes might make statements inadmissible in court but some have served me spectacularly well.

Every time I was with her and needed to test myself I'd say "Time to check my blood sugar, Sugar." Though "Sugar" never became a regular spoken endearment between us, amusing ourselves, we both took to saying that second "Sugar" at all the appropriate times. Since I check anywhere from 7-10 times each day that phrase became one of our beloved taglines.

We both loved playing with language. We adopted faux English accents when we were perplexed or confused. We'd then occasionally proceed to have entirely ridiculous conversations in bad Oxbridge. The pattern started with Tracy who was enamored with all things British. The spoiled kids in Willy Wonka's Chocolate Factory were a favorite source. "Daddy, I want an oompa loompa! I want an Oompa Loompa now!" Her whining plea always made us laugh. When one of us would lose a sock or she'd misplace her glasses her common refrain was "It's a mystery of inexhaustible contemplation." When I asked her if she'd had enough for dinner she'd answer "plenty" but in a Midwestern dialect, leaving off the T. "I've had plenny. Pliny the Elder." We took high-minded approaches and applied them to the most mundane circumstances to delight in the silly.

The first time Tracy heard me use the expression "days of yore" she laughed herself dippy. She rightly considered me a fountain of anachronisms. I love the praise "bee's knees" and rollick in "cut a rug" and "trip the light fantastic." I call unacquainted women "dear" and "sweetheart" and still say "howdy" when I meet strangers. "Howdy" came about from a decision I made when I was 19. I liked how people in rural Champaign and surrounding counties spoke. There was something warmer and friendlier about "howdy" than "hi" or "hello." I've consciously chosen most of my lifelong habits of expression. When I write the numeral seven I still cross it in the European style because it seems clearer and more sophisticated. I made that decision at 15 after we lived in Germany. It only seemed sensible to continue. I use outdated 60s expressions like "hip" and 70s expressions like "be well." Though I note that "cool," which dates from the 50s and I also use, never seems to go out of style. In short, I'm a repository for every out of date linguistic expression I ever ran across that I found cool or useful. I love how this amused Tracy—she, the great lover of language and lucid expression.

We loved sharing misspellings found in high places and low, bemoaned the firing of the world's proofreaders, sighed at the loss of erudition in common speech, cringed and laughed at malapropisms. When people disdain the snootiness of the educated classes we're pretty much what they have in mind. We used to cringe every time we heard the word "relatable" when that instance of Valley Girl Speak first entered the language. She took to saying "Whatevs" in answer to questions that deserved humorous, vague responses. She did it first ironically, then eventually, like the best of us, somewhat sincerely. We used to count how many times people used "like" in a sentence. We'd share examples of writers who forgot the grace and clarity of simple periods. Or who never understood how a semi-colon might come in handy. And people who used exclamation points all the time! OMG!

We never understood how people could dash off emails or texts inviting, through errors of spelling or logic, more questions than they ever answered. We were fastidious in wanting communication to be respectful and clear. We prided ourselves in writing emails that were proofread, grammatically impeccable, spelled correctly, devoid of as many possible future confusions and needed clarifications as possible. Not doing so felt commensurate with the level of care and attention many people bring to relationships in general these days. Little to none. That judgment probably moves us to the head of the line of old-fogeydom. Fine.

We loved playing verbal word games, riffing on a noun and sling shooting it into ridiculous new contexts, conjugating a verb surreally, or catapulting verb tenses into the wrong time zone. I love to say "Praise da Laudanum!" But I was never foolish enough to challenge her at real word games like Scrabble or Boggle. I have way too much vanity for that. I don't take loss gladly and won't readily set myself up for defeat. I don't know if the tradition started with Tracy's Mom but her whole family seemed to delight in those games. It was a tradition passed on to her daughters who, come holiday time, used to engage in quietly fierce battles of Boggle. I prefer word games like Fictionary where the absurdist in me can take flight. I would rather maximize laughs than my score.

To amuse myself, I used to ask her to say the Yiddish word "tuchas." She never mastered the ch, roiling deep in the throat. She'd say "took-us" with a hard K. I found it hilarious. This is what they mean by the dangers of miscegenation. Classic east coast Yiddish is lost on a Catholic Kansas girl. Clearly you have to be bred in hard urban environments to get it right. Thank god she wasn't. It's something I should've recorded her saying. Someone could've built a whole Seinfeld episode out of that pronunciation.

Her back gave her much pain in her final years. Starting in her breasts, the cancer first spread to the vertebrae. She'd get up from sitting or lying down and note how steely her back was. Poker faced, she'd say, "I got a stiffie."

There was a period when Tracy and I would mark the end of each day by saying "Another day over, another day closer to death." Like most taglines that couples adopt, we continued the practice as long as we could wring merriment from it, then discarded it. No doubt, there's a threshold moment in any relationship when that statement suddenly becomes too real. Fortunately, we never crossed that doorway.

She was always shy about using her Spanish. I never understood why. It always sounded great to me. But then I don't speak it. In Barcelona, in San Francisco's Mission, with our house cleaner...there were ample opportunities for her but she seemed too self-conscious to use it. She didn't like to do things less than masterfully.

There was a moment when I needed her to use her Spanish during a recording session for the narration of my film *Journey from Zanskar*. We were in the Hamptons in New York in August. Ordinarily, Tracy rarely traveled with me. She didn't like to travel much and, for reasons I'll explain later, my work usually held little direct appeal. I told her on this particular trip I was going to work with Richard Gere. "I'll come!" She volunteered before I could even pop the question. It was a lovely opportunity for us to celebrate our 6TH wedding anniversary. If I'd been a more successful filmmaker and worked with more celebrities I might have gotten her to join me on more trips.

I booked the only sound studio I could find in the Hamptons—a small in-law unit in the backyard of a quaint B&B. Not your average million dollar Hollywood recording studio. It was one of the hottest days of summer, close to 100 degrees. We had poor Richard cloistered in an un-ventilated, un-air-conditioned cubicle. He would burst out on occasion gasping for air, dripping with sweat. In keeping with typical Warrior Films budgets, for this heroic service he was paid nada.

Then the leaf blowers arrived. Did I mention the booth wasn't soundproof? I did my best to indicate that I'd like the crew to stop. That didn't seem to work. So I asked Tracy if she'd speak to them in Spanish. She was reluctant. Maybe she didn't know how to say "leaf blower" in Spanish. With barely a hesitation, Richard jumped into the fray. His Spanish sounded pretty good to me. But what might've impressed the workers more was his IMDB rating. I remember the blower's face—startled, amused, impressed. It's not every day you get asked by Richard Gere to stop working and please let the yard go to waste. In your native language no less.

Full disclosure: I might never have asked her to marry me were it not for medical insurance. I was a patient of the San Francisco Free Clinic at the time. I loved everything about that place. They had the most generous and helpful doctors, nurses, and staff. They did everything this side of the law not only to deliver quality free health care but to get their patients free prescription meds. Yet I knew the strategy of receiving long-term medical care from them was not sustainable. I needed to cover my emergency medical expenses out of pocket. If I ever required long term hospital care that too would be a personal expense. I also reasoned that as a "middle class" patient I was taking away a coveted, rare slot at the clinic that could've been used by someone in greater need. I felt guilty. So securing medical insurance from a potential partner was certainly on my relationship radar.

Tracy had it. As a tenured professor at USF her spousal benefits package was generous. (By the draconian standards of today, absolutely magnificent.) It not only included great medical, dental and eyeglass care, it also allowed me regular use of the library and free use of the huge indoor swimming pool. It afforded me opportunities to join her and colleagues on writing retreats at Sea Ranch in Sonoma County where USF owned a residence, and later to take a teaching stint with her in Budapest. It put me at the top of the list to receive invitations to teach USF screenwriting courses. I also got to be "eye candy," to accompany her to frequent USF social events and convocations.

Marriage fulfilled my need for a strategic partnership. I had fears about getting older and being able to care for myself. I also knew that as an artist my income was uneven at best and Dickensian at worst. I wanted to build sustainability into my future. By today's Western standards where romance is usually deemed decisive, it sounds almost Machiavellian to be cognizant of these intentions going into a relationship. But they were part of the equation for me. I made the right decision in every way.

Between us we had the perfect confluence of circumstances. I had matured enough to be ready for marriage and she had wizened enough to settle for nothing less. She had been married before, had birthed two daughters, and understood the gravitas that marriage requires. She didn't want to get married just to cover the legalities of me getting medical insurance. She wanted the real deal, perhaps more so in the wake of her immediately prior relationship with her boyfriend. She wanted a solid commitment from her partner. I was grateful that at 47 I had enough sense to finally look somewhere other than the edifice of sex to build a relationship on.

It took over a year from when we met, a full four months after we married, for us to move in together. We tried to find a new place. We wanted a three-bedroom apartment, one that would provide us with separate offices. Though it was Fall 2003 and San Francisco was still reeling from the 2000 bottoming-out of the tech industry, we couldn't find anything workable, affordable, and within easy walking distance of USF. It was the same San Francisco real estate market—less crazy than before, but still crazy. So I ended up giving up my own treasured studio apartment in the Mission and moved into her smaller, more workable apartment in the Lower Haight. Since she already had an office on campus she was gracious enough to offer me the "2ND bedroom" for my office. Though I was grateful for a separate space with a closable door, my office was little more than a walk-in closet with a window on to the neighbor's dirty gray wall two feet away. What remained of her own home office—a small folding table, really—she moved into our tiny living room. I'm convinced that the reason why I never heard again from a movie producer friend of mine who I invited to dinner with his wife one night was that they saw how shabbily we were living compared to their grand house in the Berkeley hills. That event might also account for my lasting "guest fright" at having film professionals and other successful colleagues over for dinner. Fuck 'em. Though small, I loved that place I shared with Tracy for the simple reason she was in it.

Before meeting her, I had reduced what initially was a very long list of wants in a partner to three essentials.

1. *A woman who is deeply knowing of herself, who she is, and her place in the world.* Tracy was a mother, a professor, and a writer. She loved those roles. She wasn't seeking something more or different, unlike most of the women I had known and loved. And unlike myself.

2. *A woman who has a strong spiritual or religious practice.* This point, arguably, is a subset of the one above. It's important to me that a partner situates herself in the universe in a way that makes sense to her, that is a source of knowing and comfort, providing a living antidote to cynicism. None of my former partners fit this bill. But "belief" or "faith" is not enough. It's important to me that a partner have a strong spiritual *practice*, something she does regularly, to keep that knowing tuned, to support her through the times of confusion and challenge. As a recovering Catholic, Tracy was no longer interested in organized religion. She had recently discovered meditation and was an

avid practitioner. Though she never called herself a Buddhist she was drawn to the logic and practice of the teachings. We occasionally sat and meditated together in the mornings, including the very first morning of our married life together. Following the requisite though not overlong celebratory Bacchanal, she got up with me at six to join the Green Gulch Zen Center community for morning service. I deeply appreciated that. I thought it a great start to our relationship. But her practice was never sustained and that disappointed me. Of course, I too regularly abandoned my practice, begun in 1988, to veer off into Sephardic deserts of neurosis, remaking myself into a Wandering Jew in search of meaning when all I needed was to return to the simplicity of a practice proven effective and long established. In her last year, Tracy took to visiting the Oakland Cathedral of Christ the Light, a few blocks from our house. She loved the space itself and the trimmings of ritual—the incense and candles—but couldn't stomach the dogma and stopped going.

3. *A woman who is committed to working on herself and the relationship.* Self-improvement is important to me. "Those not busy being born are busy dying," Bob Dylan memorably sang. 21 years of men's work, preceded by ten years of therapy—intensive for the first two years, occasional for the following eight—convinced me of the mountain of work I needed to do to become the man I wanted to be. I expect no less from my partner. I know that no problem is irresolvable if she is willing to do her own work and willing to do our work together as a couple. It's unremarkable to note that every relationship runs into problems eventually. What's less commonly observed is that, once tested, every relationship succeeds or fails not on how much "love" the partners have for each other but on how committed they are to working through their differences. In-

tegrity and accountability count for much more in successful relationships than anything pertaining to passion or romance. Tracy and I saw a therapist for a period of time to try to work through our sex issue. Though the visits never resolved the conflict they did clarify where our differences lay, which I'll return to in a moment. Tracy also got sustenance from various circles. She was an active member of many different support groups for women with cancer, outliving everyone in her first San Francisco circle, most of the women in her second LA circle, and then dying herself during her third circle in Oakland. We did couples workshops together and we co-founded two couples support groups. She also participated in the powerful "HER" weekend workshop for women. When she learned that the workshop was staffed by men as well as women it scared her so much she felt obligated to attend in order to confront her fear. She returned a woman reborn. "Get ready. Your Warrior Woman is coming home!" she shouted into the phone on her drive back. She was humble enough to know that she had plenty to learn and improve upon. And, like most married people, the last person she wanted to hear that from was her spouse.

So Tracy had my three primary relationship requisites covered. Handily. So sex? Was it a problem? Yes. Did it sink our beautiful marriage? Not even close.

When it comes to sexuality I subscribe to David Deida's notion of polarity. Opposite energies create sexual dynamism. We didn't make love often in our final years together. "Did you take a vow of celibacy sometime that you didn't tell me about?" she asked. "Sort of," I replied sheepishly. My issue was a lack of sexual heat. I didn't feel much with her. "Do you think we'll ever have sex again?" Stupidly and insufficiently I said, "Hope springs eternal." "It takes more than hope," she coolly replied. Yes, it does. But I felt entirely stuck and didn't know how to respond in a way that simply wasn't going to rehash what we both already knew.

In the few months we were dating, before I asked her to marry me, I asked if she was hit on a lot by lesbians. She seemed surprised by the question and said no. "Why do you ask?" Then it was my turn to be surprised. "Because you have a lot of 'masculine' energy." These days of course we put "masculine" in quotes because the continuum of energy with pliant and open at one end and hard and tough at the other is no longer ascribed in gender terms and rightly so. But for me there was something "manly" about Tracy that affected my sex drive. Though I prized her assuredness, her toughness and poise in the greater world, and valued those qualities at home in our daily interaction and conversation, the very same attributes left me cold in the arousal department. She was physically striking and had an amazing, sexy body, but her choices in clothes, hairstyle, and bedroom demeanor were chemically ineffective for me. In fact, they were a turn-off. My dick doesn't motivate through intellect. I don't get hard once I drop more deeply into Simone Beauvoir's *Second Sex*. I became the poster boy for the separation of hormones and intellect and resigned myself to making love on average only once or twice a month.

So many relationships start with and get built upon that raw surge of energy, that animal attraction. Not ours. Before marrying, I remember saying that given how much I loved and admired so many aspects of who she was I could easily do without the heat. I also fessed up to my sexual history. I tend to lose interest in my partners 1-2 years into relationships. This was the first relationship I ever chose knowing it was wise and sustainable rather than "I can't wait to get into this woman's pants." And with Tracy I could have it both ways. She was still a very beautiful woman—very easy on the eyes and, for me, her potential partner, a huge bolster to my occasionally fragile ego for us to be seen together publicly.

So sex was a source of dissatisfaction and disillusionment for us both. It was mostly my fault. She was more turned on by me than I was by her. She just didn't harp on it. And after a while we both made sure the subject didn't arise.

I took to buying her clothes. It wasn't really conscious on my part, at least initially, but I wanted to put her in clothes that I found sexy. Some things I bought her she liked and wore happily. Hippie-style shirts for example. But most things she laughed off as ridiculous and age-inappropriate, like sexy stockings and longer flowing skirts or shorter, tighter ones. "Your hoochie-coochie tastes," she called them. She preferred sensible pants and shirts, jackets and shoes, clothes she considered smart. I found them plain unattractive.

After her death a number of former students (all males) commented on how sexy she was. I can well imagine being a 19 year old in her classroom and feeling much the same. It saddens me to think that her sex appeal might largely have been lost on me due to age. Though Tracy was somewhat of an exception being only 18 months younger than me, I confess it's rare to find myself attracted to women my age or older. If that makes me the poster boy for elder stage sexism so be it. It's real. I won't analyze or defend it.

When we first met I bought her a used leather jacket she said she liked but never wore. In the year before she died I tried to buy her cowboy boots. We could never find a pair that fit her properly or that looked great to both of us, though we only tried one store. She committed to searching online but she didn't maintain an interest long enough to find anything suitable. In my no doubt sexist view I think she would've been one hell of a knockout in the right skirt and blouse, cowboy boots and leather jacket. Alas, I never got to see her in them.

She didn't want me to touch her in suggestive ways when we were out in public, like touching her ass. That too was a loss for me. I find expressions of sexual interest in public erotic. A similar aspect of control extended to the bedroom. "This way, but not this way; here, but not here..." That also cooled my abandon. Whether in public or back home, I began to fear doing something she wouldn't like or doing something the wrong way. Result? I retreated from her physically even further. Most couples nowadays—gay, straight, whatever—seem implicitly to understand these issues. I was a "top" and she was, well, she wasn't quite a "top" too. She liked both. Frankly, *I* like both. But somehow feeling like my top energy was thwarted undermined the whole proposition.

I know a lot of her sexual behavior had to do with childhood, suffering sexual abuse from her father. I'm sure she was attacked plenty working as a teen on the night shift at Denny's. She was also sexually harassed as a junior professor in the English department when she first arrived at USF in 1993. Maybe that was the time she finally decided she needed to take a strong public stand. Though it was a long process and extremely painful for her, putting her on the losing side of support from many colleagues, she successfully sued the university and put an end to it. At least from one principal perpetrator. Though that was years before I met her, I was retroactively extremely proud of her. The whole ordeal might have been critical for her, tremendously advancing her own growth—a coming out party only a few years after her divorce to celebrate her independence and power as a woman. Perhaps it also helped exorcise past demons. But for life in an institution that eventually became most beloved, it was a painful start.

No doubt she considered sex play the domain of the bedroom, behind locked doors and only with those most trusted. In a way that was perhaps symbolic of that exterior/interior distinction, that top/bottom dynamic, underneath her unrevealing and to me, unattractive clothes, she wore extremely sexy underwear. I loved those panties and kept some favorite pairs.

I sometimes wonder if limited lovemaking didn't contribute to her death. My readings about sex, almost all completed long ago in my 20s, lead me to believe that the body, especially the female body, needs and deserves regular sex in order to maintain good health and peak performance. Eastern practices tend to prescribe regular orgasms for women, the more the better, and generally fewer orgasms, with very selective ejaculations for men. In fact, the goal for mindful men is to have orgasms without ejaculation, which, after much conscious effort with my girlfriend in our early 20s, I was able to experience once. Would regular and better lovemaking have contributed to a longer life for Tracy? Perhaps. She certainly deserved more.

Long before I met Tracy I just got lazy and stopped practicing what I learned in my 20s from Jolan Chang, author of THE TAO OF LOVE AND SEX. I know I shouldn't have more than 4-5 orgasms a month. My health can't take it. Ejaculations tend to set my immune system back. I rarely get colds but almost invariably when I do it's 2-3 days following ejaculation. In the early days of our marriage Tracy told me she occasionally masturbated. In later years I stopped asking.

My shadow played into our sex dynamic too. My own controller, my own perpetrator...I knew that not making love hurt. She wanted and deserved all my love, including sexual love. I wasn't going to give it to her. Not on her terms, so not at all. There it is—shameful and real. I consigned myself to jerking off 2-3 times a month watching porn. She knew I did this. Like everything else, we discussed it. The agreement we made was around limits, basically to make sure I didn't become an addict. We even watched together a few times to stimulate our own lovemaking. Though it temporarily helped, neither of us were motivated enough to make it a sustaining practice.

Sensing most of this in advance, I thought still wanting to marry her a mature decision to make. Tracy made for the most wonderful partner in nearly every way. Giving up notions of perfection seemed like progress. Since I knew that trouble arose in every relationship, what mattered less to me than the facts of our "incompatibilities" was the truth of our willingness to work through anything and accept everything. There can be perfection within imperfection. For me, this is that story.

The first New Year's Eve we shared together was 2002. I didn't have a couch or love seat so we sat on the floor of my apartment. It may have been the first time Tracy undertook co-creating ritual with a romantic partner. But when I broached the subject she was open and ready.

We lit a candle. We named everything we wanted to let go of from the previous year. She had plenty to put behind her. The year began with her diagnosis of cancer. It proceeded through her boyfriend leaving her for another woman he believed he had impregnated. She moved out of the home she shared with him and dearly loved. She experienced all of Western medicine's standard cancer treatments—surgery, radiation, chemo. She moved a second time when she couldn't take the all-night pounding of the dance club next door. Her entire world basically crumbled around her. She had plenty to bury.

My year had also been challenging. My recent film *The Unspoken* had flopped and my newest one *Boys to Men?* seemed to be headed in the same direction. I spent over $7,000 to rid myself of diabetes by working with a Chinese doctor administering incredibly painful foot treatments. For 20 minutes she took a stick and jammed it into multiple discrete and sensitive locations in my feet. I folded a towel and stuffed it in my mouth to muffle the screams. I did this 3-4 days a week. On off days, I had a hard, molded plastic mat with "pebbles" of different sizes that I would walk on for 20 minutes. My diet was limited to a regimen of vegetables and a little rice and tofu. I lost about 15 pounds on my already thin frame. Although I felt virtuous, I succeeded only in reserving a special place for myself in Fools Heaven. By year's end, I began to resign myself to living out my days as an insulin dependent diabetic.

I wish I remembered more about what we each shared that night. Regardless, the ceremony didn't last long. We had known each other for only a month. I proposed to her within two more months. We did a round of what new things we wanted to welcome into our lives. Aside from the usual requests for changes in work fortunes, for me that meant love and a new relationship. I don't remember if Tracy mentioned our relationship at that time. But she never hesitated when it came to welcoming it into her life. We clearly understood that there was one predominant factor that united us—mortality. We each knew life was short and we wanted to maximize every moment of it. To us, most people appeared delusional since they seemed unwilling or unable to understand this. We knew the clock was ticking.

Recognizing her smarts, organizational talents, and leadership qualities, within a week or two of meeting her I plotted to make her the producer of my films. I thought we could use our wonderful relationship as a platform to conquer the film world. Clearly, I wasn't alone in that judgment. I soon learned that only one year prior she had co-written and produced a short fiction film with her former lover. So she politely demurred. She had already experienced that particular set of headaches and felt once was sufficient. Her refusal to me might have been further colored by her personal experience with P. But I was dogged...so she repeatedly demurred. She was willing to be supportive of my work but only within strict parameters. Eventually she stepped on to my Warrior

Films' Board and served a number of years as Secretary. The entire time we were together she also served invaluably as my deepest confidante and advisor. But I never stopped teasing her about what a successful film producing team we could've been.

That's why it pierced my heart when, three weeks after her death, I was informed by HR at USF that there was a Tracy Seeley retirement account earmarked for Warrior Films. The sum of $68,400 had been donated to my company. I found this astonishing. Tracy and I discussed all her retirement accounts and how the money in them was to be divided equally between her two daughters and myself. But she never spoke a word about this one. In March 2016, during the run-up to her death, she made final adjustments to all her retirement accounts except this one, which remained unchanged since 2003.

2003! The very year we married, mere months after we met, she determined this account should be donated to Warrior Films. She committed those funds at the exact time we were having those producing conversations and she was saying no. Then she kept it secret from me for 13 years. She wanted it to be a parting gift. More than a gift, she wanted it to be a blessing from beyond the grave to continue on with my work, work she knew caused me no end of self-doubt, of anxiety and heartbreak. Time and again I would pour my heart out to her. She would listen and say quietly, "I wish I could do more." Though I occasionally still teased her about producing, not once did she betray an inkling of the gift she had in store for me on her death. If that's not elegance and class, not to mention generosity, I don't know what is.

I admit that I took advantage of her generosity whenever I flew with her. She would take a middle seat leaving me the aisle or window. A corporeal emblem of true love. With my long legs I would invariably take all my own space and usurp some of hers. That's no small gift from a woman herself six feet tall. When I occasionally regaled her with stories of traveling first class in the wake of *Hoop Dreams'* success she never became wistful that I had fallen so far from grace. She never let on that she minded. But I minded. A man wants his woman to feel like a Queen. To be properly attended, accorded all the rights and privileges of sovereignty. When those opportunities arose she certainly relished them—a fancy hotel room, a lavish dinner out, riding in a Town Car. I felt remorse, even shame, at not being able to share that kind of success with her. I don't think we ever rode a limo together. She wasn't strong enough to accompany me to Sundance in 2014. Healthy, she would have loved going to film festivals, award ceremonies and dinners, and would have felt at home in that world.

Though we nurtured each other regularly through sickness and health, no episode stands out more to me than when I got poison oak on our first road trip together in the summer of 2003. This was before we were married, only six months after we met. We were visiting her daughter in Eugene, OR, truck camping in the "white palace"—my all white Chevy 1500 WT. Complete with an 8-foot extended bed, a camper shell, and permanently installed queen futon in the back, we could drop anchor anywhere, crawl in the back and sleep like royalty. Add a couple bikes and a cooler and we could go for days—Yosemite, Lake Tahoe, Big Sur, Redwood National Forest, Mendocino, Mt. Lassen, Mt. Shasta…and we did, most of those places on this one trip.

I headed out jogging from her daughter's house one morning. I used to love exploring neighborhoods that way. Her place was semi-rural so I was enjoying the back roads on an early summer day. Before long I needed to take a crap. I hate when that happens. Usually I'll wait until I've moved my bowel before heading out but this morning I forgot. The country was wide open but I found a large shaded yard, shielded from both street and house by large trees. A nice green spot with lots of little plants. You know where this is going...

Being from the Midwest I was quite familiar with poison ivy. But not so much with poison oak. I tore off handfuls to wipe myself clean and happily resumed my run. It took about two days for things to start getting uncomfortable. We were driving the Columbia River Gorge. I could barely sit still. Finally, it dawned on me what I'd done. We pulled into a rest stop and commandeered a bathroom. I dropped my trousers, bent over, and spread my legs for Tracy to take a look. This is not what I recommend to young couples for building intimacy. She confirmed the worst. After she finished laughing she was extremely sympathetic. When I wasn't in oatmeal baths, I spent much of the next ten days having Tracy apply various ointments to my inflamed butt cheeks and painfully aggrieved anus. Though it made a great story to tell at diverse social gatherings, it amply demonstrated to me how Tracy was an unafraid, sympathetic, and able caretaker. Fortunately, in time, I was able to return the favor.

She was by instinct and training a mother. She loved raising and caring for her daughters. She had no interest in mothering the man she loved, certainly not me, especially after her previous boyfriend. When our relationship commenced, she was very clear about never knitting me sweaters or baking me pies. She never darned my socks, sewed buttons, or patched pants. "Throw 'em way," she'd say. She was clear that her career as a domestic was over, even if housekeeping took a few more years to give up. Still, she had natural caretaking tendencies that she couldn't shake. When I left home somehow forgetting my insulin or test strips she'd overnight them to me. If I needed some data from my desktop computer she would forward it. If there were houseguests coming that I couldn't be there to meet she would handle it. In the kitchen she kept everything functional, ready, and in good order.

I care a lot about household aesthetics. I don't care about nor am skilled at fixing and maintaining household objects. She tended to all that. She also cooked most of the meals, paid and instructed the housecleaners, rearranged pictures and furniture, framed photos and art, bought food, litter and toys for the cat, and tidied up after guests…All I took care of was the car and the garbage. I didn't realize it because it all happened slowly and "organically." But I fell asleep to the management of my own existence and came to rely on her caretaking. She stepped into the vacuum and assumed control. Or perhaps she simply asserted the control that she presumed was hers. Without realizing it was happening I let her take care of me. Despite what I had written in the Salon.com personals I let her mother me.

This fed right into my shadow. My key relationship wound is not being honored and acknowledged as a man. No doubt hearkening back to my experience at nine of becoming "the man of the house," if I don't receive that recognition I will project unwanted mothering on to women. The very caretaking I have defaulted on providing for myself I will accuse them of unnecessarily providing for me. I never trusted my mother's compliments because I told myself that's what mothers do. It doesn't mean anything; it's her job. Mothers are supposed to say nice things to boys. Not projecting that sentiment on to spouses and lovers is a challenge, I believe, for most men. Not a prospect for sustaining a healthy relationship.

We were aware of the challenges of projecting the wounding behaviors of our parents on to one another. At her worst, Tracy's behavior felt emasculating to me. She would discount what I had to say and dismiss me as uninformed, ridicule my expressions of speech, and disparage my understanding and use of household implements, particularly in the kitchen. For her part, she sometimes felt discounted and unimportant to me, like she hardly mattered. She also received far less of the physical contact with me that she desired.

As a remedy, Tracy and I often resolved to do the candle ceremony every day. That ceremony is designed for mutual expression of the necessary, self-designed endearments, putting balm on longstanding bruises. Tracy's core pain had to do with not being cherished. I'd take her hands, look her in the eye, and say, "Tracy I treasure you." Tracy would do the equivalent of focusing on my deepest suffering, saying "Frederick, I acknowledge and honor you for the man you are."

A mentor once pointed out to me how important it is to accept commendations gracefully. It still isn't easy for me, though I've worked hard to step into gratitude and magnanimity. Perhaps fortunately, the praise doesn't come as often anymore, at least from the world of filmmaking. Tracy recognized my tendency to downplay affirmation and was woman enough for the challenge. It was one more aspect of her character that augmented her Queenly presence. On days when we didn't do the formal candle ceremony, she'd still look me in the eye, sometimes taking my hands, to make her acknowledgements known and felt. My default mode is to deflect, shake my head, to disabuse. She'd repeat herself. Sometimes I'd squirm. So she'd say it again, often for the third time. "I honor you for the good man you are." On my good days, I learned to breathe, take it all in, and say "thank you." Now I can sit more comfortably in the discomfort of those moments. The irony is I believe every man longs to hear some version of that statement from his wife, if only once in his lifetime. Tracy offered it to me regularly.

Who holds healthy sovereign energy are not idle concerns for me, especially since it's found all too scarcely in Western societies today. Robert Moore's neo-Jungian work tells us that these Sovereign/Warrior/Magician/Lover archetypal energies reside in all of us and that it's our job to manifest them fully and in balance. Part of why so many men who do the ManKind Project training consider it their long overdue initiation into mature masculinity, as did I, is because these archetypal energies awake in them.

My MKP weekend most nourished my Lover, giving me license to unlock and express a long-repressed flood of emotions, first in the inviolable company of other MKP men, and eventually with the general public. Historically, as an artist and would-be intellect, I'd operated most comfortably from the Magician quadrant, using my thinking brain and creativity to manifest what I wanted. I was ruthless in protecting my ability to create and be "free." I severed any and all relationships I perceived as unconducive to my work and growth. I never wanted to get married and I certainly didn't want to be tied down with kids. Following graduate school, I broke up with my girlfriend not because there was anything wrong with her but because I was off to my next great life adventure—moving to China—and my plans didn't include her. I was a Romantic and discovery was my Muse. My Magician reigned supreme while my Warrior and King functioned more like Savage and Tyrant, when they functioned at all.

In time I learned my greatest work was to bring my Warrior and Sovereign out of the shadows, to make them fully and purposefully operational. Making room in my "kingdom" for Tracy's family, which was always her desire, was a stretch. Making Tracy herself an object of commensurate attention with my work was also no small challenge. A challenge that was only fully met in the months leading up to her death.

My Lover actually stands in the way. I can be lazy and complacent, seduced by abundant distractions. Commenting on my sweet tooth, a friend once rightly noted that I have a weakness for the sweet things in life. I suppose everybody shares this vice to some degree. Of course, for a diabetic it can prove fatal. But he meant it in the broadest sense of life fulfillment, including heart to heart connections, joyous occasions, and career successes. Like addicts and near-addicts everywhere, my predilection for all things sweet makes it hard to withstand the inexorable grind of daily life. That persistent draw to pleasure, to fulfillment, is an over inflation of my Lover. The lure of the feeling state is too strong, and of course the most satisfying feeling is pleasure. I get pleasure from socializing and deep, heartfelt connections. If I'm not careful I'll put way too many social events on my calendar and run from pain, felt or feared.

I first became aware of this in my teen years when I was known as Ann Landers to my fellow schoolmates. I would listen gladly to anyone's emotional distress in order to build trust and friendship. Yes, there was voyeurism involved. Yes, I was trying to understand and resolve my own emotional needs by addressing theirs. But that was all unconscious. Consciously, I had goodwill and thought it easy to bear witness to their suffering and offer helpful suggestions. This character trait has proven to be popular with women. No less so with Tracy. Though she occasionally had to remind me not to try to fix her in any way, she always appreciated my ready empathy.

One sign of maturity is the ability to withstand the pull of immediate pleasure, of immediate connection, for the greater good of persisting with aloneness, hardship or pain. The best way to counteract my overactive Lover is with my engaged Warrior. My Warrior has to be constantly on guard and ready to intervene at any time with fierce clarity and determination. Saying no, setting boundaries, not giving in, staying focused on work and tasks at hand, not getting distracted by parties or the pull of others' emotional needs. Though I still default to Magician and Lover energies, I've done a fair job embodying healthy Warrior and Sovereign energies to counterbalance them. I stay disciplined in doing my work, and remain focused on long-term intentions. It's no accident my company is named Warrior Films. My "kingliness" is further borne out in how I perceived Tracy. It takes an awakened sovereign to recognize a fellow sovereign. Leaders recognize leaders.

Tracy was a true Queen. Though I was aware of her abundant sovereign energy at the time of our wedding I couldn't articulate it so simply. Dozens of the cards and letters I've received since her death speak to her august bearing. "I remember her regal, wise, and gentle presence" is par for the course. None of the other partners I've had in my lifetime—all beautiful, intelligent, compassionate, creative women—pass this singular threshold. Mostly because of their unwillingness to do their own emotional work. In her sovereignty, Tracy towered above them all.

I tend to judge heterosexual men by the women they partner with. Especially older men. If they have trophy wives—younger, prettier versions of their previous partners, or perhaps foreign, more subservient wives—that says a lot. How many men, 40 and up, truly have Queens? Tough, wise, efficacious women who not only can stand up to what the world dishes out but can stand up to them? Sadly, not many. It's usually indicative of a sovereign wound in the man himself. He usually has a deflated or inflated sovereign. Either one can make him desire a woman who is less than his equal—usually playing the role of whore, maid or mother. Getting all three is winning the trifecta of conventional manhood. But men can also desire "equals" who only succeed in matching their deflated sovereign—confidantes or buddies, friends rather than fellow commanders. I see this a lot with younger people today, often more pals with each other than comrade leaders in life's noble struggle. Sovereignty at its simplest means the ability to translate one's compassion and brilliance into wise action to serve the greatest good.

I can usually tell within five minutes of meeting women where their male partners fall on the sovereignty index. The woman's age and beauty relative to her man are important markers, but there are more. Is the woman as smart or smarter than he is? Is she well spoken? Does she carry herself with self-assurance and pride? Does she express her own needs or defer to her husband's? Does she stand comfortably in her own power? Or does her husband speak for her, finishing her every sentence? A man in sovereign balance wants a real partner—someone he knows he can be true to and will be true to him, who will have his back. Together they can plot a course for well-being not only for the kingdom within—their mental and physical health, their home, their family—but for the kingdom without—the extended family, the places of work, the neighborhood, the communities of choice, and, by extension, the well-being of the planet. Together they can fulfill the sovereign imperative and realize their deepest authenticity and greatest joy.

This was the unspoken substance of many of our conversations. "What is best here? What is the maximal good?" That was the common, high ground Tracy and I walked together. Particularly with her family, Tracy asked me for help. She asked me to offer mentorship to the husband of one of her daughters who was fatherless and never had a positive long-term relationship with a man his entire life. We also counseled each other about work challenges. For years Tracy told me to adapt my *Boys Become Men* project to include women and girls, both to improve my chances to secure funding and to deflect charges of sexism. I helped her bury the hatchet when some insecure colleagues in her department went on the warpath to ban "literature professors" like her from teaching creative writing. Even when we disagreed on politics we always came back to the fundamental question "What is the highest good we can do here?"

In her self-assurance and clarity about what's best, she always blessed my work with and for men. In January 1996, I staffed a ManKind Project weekend with my brother Larry. There was a staff member from Wisconsin who explained he was there because his wife told him "it's time for you to go be with the men." It was winter. Both of them were a bit stir crazy. His wife, in her wisdom, in her sovereignty, recognized he was growing impatient and testy with her, driving her batty. Tracy had a similar ability to recognize when I needed to be with the men. She never begrudged me going because she knew the man she got back was always more loving and patient than the one who left. She never understood women who resisted having their men attend personal growth trainings solely with other men. She thought they were acting against their own best interest, denying themselves the better men they said they always wanted. That's why I always loved it when Tracy attended our MKP Homecoming Ceremonies. In one such celebration, she stood up in front of 100 people and publicly thanked the men there for doing their emotional work. She felt safer as a woman because of it and expressed gratitude on behalf of herself, her daughters and her sisters.

The blessings we shared with each other ran in both directions. In the wake of reviewing dozens of items from our history together, I ran across a note I wrote to Tracy in LA May 7, 2007, while on her way to the HER weekend, which I reprint here verbatim:

Well,

This is odd. Here I am at home. You're not in the other room; you're out at your drawing class. I suppose it should be easier to write you when you're not clicking and clacking on your keyboard, or plucking the guitar strings, or silently drawing. (What else do you do out there? ;-) But feeling your presence nearby feels like it would make it easier. That's what I tell myself anyway.

I wanted to add my voice to the chorus of acknowledgement and love I hope you're hearing and reveling in at this workshop. Though I'm clear about feeling intimidated for the task. It's a lesson I first learned no doubt when my Dad disappeared forever out of my life at 9. I'm referring to my commitment to be perpetually up to date, to speak my truth ALL THE TIME to those I love. I feel like I do that with you. It's part of my commitment to you. So even though I want to do it now, I don't feel like I have a lot that's new to say.

Mostly I just want to tell you what a joy it is to see you every day. I love your sense of humor; yes, OK, even if half the time I don't get it. More to the point, I love your readiness and willingness to laugh. There's a lot that's truly hilarious in this world and I love you pointing it out to me and I to you. Making you laugh is truly one of my life's greatest joys. Thank you for returning that gift to me so readily!

More than your laughter, I relish your shining presence. And I'm not using a metaphor. You shine. Glow. Sparkle. I don't know what it is—your diet, your sabbatical year off... I truly don't know. But over the last year you've truly started to shine and it's a joy to behold. YOU'RE a joy to behold. Even when you say you're down, like you were during your cold. You still were shining alive! Have your friends like Karen noticed? Your support group? Am I crazy?! I tell my men's circle about it all the time and shake my head. It's a mystery to me. Let's face it—it's certainly not LA! I can't attribute it to learning guitar or drawing since it started well before, though that's a tempting explanation. Let's hope it's never solved.

You've made my home the kind of home I always wanted to live in. The kind of dream home I always HOPED I'd live in. One filled with regular, spontaneous creations of music and art. How cool is that! And it ain't me, babe. No, it ain't me babe—making the music and drawings. It's you. Thank you. Thank you for bringing your love of art and creation into our home. Thank you for stretching yourself to find that creator in you. Maybe starting your book opened the door. We all knew what a great teacher and academic writer you were. Now we can dance the dance of this different order of creation with you. What a dance! THANK YOU THANK YOU THANK YOU. There is no happier home life I could ever envision. Thank you for making my dreams come true.

Love forever, your man in the saddle,

That wasn't the only dream Tracy made come true. I always dreamed of marrying a beautiful writer. We were celebrating her book release with a combo backyard housewarming BBQ for our new Oakland home in October 2009. That's when I realized, "Hey, it came true!" I loved hearing her read from that book. I can still hear her voice in my head when I scan the words on the page. She had a lovely, melodious voice in which I could occasionally discern the slightest Kansas twang. In her last month I intended to record her reading children's stories to her grandsons. (The youngest was born three weeks after her death.) But I got the idea too late and time was already too short. Recording anything was too demanding for her few remaining moments.

I miss hearing that voice. I purposely saved a voicemail I got from her near the end, while she was in the hospital. "Hello Chumley," she began. Sing-songy, sweetly good-natured, playful. "I'm just calling to amuse you because I'm so out of it with all the drugs...I thought you'd enjoy hearing my besotted voice." Did I! It was delightful to me, and pure Tracy. So I saved it thinking "I will listen to this message after she's gone—to connect with her. It's the perfect memento and it will cheer me up." But I never told Tracy. I had it for about a week. When she got home I didn't think to mention it and she deleted it. It was so stupid of me not to tell her to save it. It breaks my heart now that I don't have that dulcet twinkling to listen to.

CHAPTER 4
"YOU'RE NOT THE BOSS OF ME!"

WITHIN 3-4 MONTHS of our meeting, I told Tracy I could already foresee the worst aspects of our future together and they looked like a mid-career Bergman movie. An older couple, stuck together on the Faroe Islands, spending their days wordlessly, staring out from gray shores into the endless gray sea on days when even the sunshine isn't bright. Not quite *Persona*, but close. My biggest fear was that we'd run out of things to say to each other and share interminable silences. That bleak vision turned out not too far off. There were more than a few days we spent together, beached.

When we'd get mad at each other we'd try to address it in adult ways; half the time we could break through and resolve things quickly. But the other half meant settling in on the stony beach and watching the icebergs drift by. We'd cohabitate and put on sweaters for the chill. We could go days—each stuck in her/his self-righteousness and hurt. Sometimes you could feel the North Sea winds blow across the dinner table.

Tracy and I both recognized that we simply didn't have enough to say to each other. We resolved to do what we could to smoke pot and drink more alcohol. Either one loosened our tongues enough so they would flap with more ease and our hearts would open. It was tricky, though, because alcohol clearly weakened her immune system and gave her hangovers. She was a delightful drunk. One glass was all it took. She got playful and silly, as do I, though I sometimes require more than one glass. But as pot smokers we were flops. We'd hack and spume, deciding it's not worth the pain. Friends recommended water pipes. We finally bought a cheap glass one seven months before she died that was broken by the time we got home. We finally had to face facts. As bon vivants, we were failures. There was too much northern European in each of us.

So there we were, two mirrors facing each other, both eager for some sign of life to suddenly appear and start dancing in the reflection of the other. Staring in hopeful expectation is not a recipe for enlivened interaction. We discussed the conundrum many times. At one point Tracy took to making notes on things we could discuss over dinner. For my part I was flummoxed by how a brilliant English professor could seemingly have so little to say about what she read. The issue was compounded by the alignment of our tastes. Whether discussing movies, or art, or music, both of us would offer our brief analyses and we would almost invariably agree. End of discussion. That polarity was missing. Ideally, we would've challenged each other more, intellectually pushing into the recesses of each other's thinking.

I craved interaction more than she did. I wanted to see more movies, plays, theater, art, concerts, lectures and talks…I also wanted the experience to stimulate us—to become a catalyst to deepen our conversations and relationship. She wasn't averse to going out but she only rarely took the lead, usually with events related to USF or friends. Other events inevitably arose that I wanted to attend. More often than not she demurred. So it was up to me to go alone or find someone else. Occasionally, that's exactly what I did. But all too often I gave into resignation and stayed home. I wanted to go with *her*. I wanted the event to be one more occasion for us to enliven our relationship with each other and the world.

The event just didn't mean as much experienced alone or with someone chosen as a substitute.

Like many an introvert I suppose, she was happy knowing I was near but she didn't necessarily need interaction. After the first month of my two-month trip to Australia in 2011, her emails became truncated. "Come home," was the entirety of more than one. But once I was home she didn't necessarily want to go out and do things, or have long intense discussions about the state of the world. She just wanted me close, near, but not necessarily physically adjacent to her. She breathed deeper and felt more secure, just knowing I was in my office in the other room, that she could come in for a hug or a brief conversation, that she could sit in my lap and if need be, cry and be held. That was peace. That was security. That was trust. She knew where to find me when the latest news from the doctor arrived. She sat on my lap crying, "I don't want to die!" I learned to be ready for anything and to accept everything. Good training in Zen.

Our conflicts would flare up very quickly and then take a long time to subside. Fortunately those North Sea interludes occurred less often and grew briefer. I know that emotional distance was painful for Tracy. For me it became physically so. I felt a constriction in my chest, squeezing the airy goodness out of me. It simply got to the point where neither of us could justify living with the pain of disconnection. It seemed profoundly, glaringly, unnecessary. One of us would apologize to the other. "That's not the man I want to be," I said a lot in the first years of our marriage. "That's not the woman I want to be," Tracy took to saying. Life can be so simple, relatively free of neurotic suffering, if people only observe saying "ouch" when they're hurt and "oops" when they hurt others. We didn't necessarily have a solution to whatever issue set us off but we chose to go forward differently because to do otherwise seemed too stupid. Occasionally we would hash out new agreements. Often those agreements were about strategies for rebuilding intimacy, like doing the candle ceremony, setting aside time each day for hugs, going out for meals and movies.

What could have been one of our toughest moments came about a year before she died. I was horny and not directing that sexual energy toward her, where even I knew it needed to go. During a walk around our beloved Lake Merritt, I asked her whether she could agree to me taking on short-term sex partners. "Here we go…" she moaned. She had long known the other shoe would eventually drop. She was understandably upset. Not only had her last boyfriend cheated on her and left her for another woman, her philanderer father destroyed her parents' marriage and broke her mother's heart. Her sister's marriage also broke up partly because her husband had an untreated sex addiction. Nothing mattered more to Tracy than fidelity.

I argued the best case I could which calmed her not at all. In my delusion I thought having an occasional fling might be a workable alternative. She didn't say "No, don't do it," but she absolutely hated the idea. Finally I said, "Look. I'm not going to do this without your approval. Period." I loved her and had no interest whatsoever in leaving her. That eased her pain somewhat. Soon thereafter, rushing off to the public bathroom in the park, I tripped over a big rock and drove two jagged edges deep into my left calf. I still carry the scars. We never officially ended the discussion but for all intents and purposes my foray into the subject of other partners was over. I didn't have sex with another woman the entire time we were together. That day might have been the last time she was physically capable of circumnavigating the lake with me.

Giving my word and following through on it means a lot to me. I was born with an inviolable sense of ethics. For me, a sense of honor is akin to what religion is for others. I knew I always wanted to "do the right thing." But it took me a long time to figure out what that meant and how to do it. I was almost 40 when I learned through MKP how to truly live in integrity and be wholly accountable as a man. When I was younger I had no clue; no one ever taught me. So being able to say I was completely faithful to her the entire 13 and a half years we were together fills me with pride. And in truth, monogamy took some self-control. There were times, particularly while traveling, when I thought about acting out. But I always had both a practical reason and a soulful one not to do it. I am terrible at deceit. That's the practical part. More importantly, I know that any infidelity would have broken her heart. I simply couldn't do that to her. Periodically she would ask me, sometimes directly, other times indirectly, whether I had affairs. I felt bigger as a man and grateful to myself that I could always look her in the eye and say, "No sweetie. Only you."

Her convictions were strong about many things, as are mine, and I adored her principles. Tracy loved going slow. She preferred taking public transportation, partly because it expressed her deeply democratic values. It's also the right thing to do environmentally and that meant a lot too. She enjoyed the prospect of meeting new people, of being entertained by unusual goings-on, common in San Francisco, either on or off the bus. She liked seeing what was happening on the street, what buildings were going up or coming down, appreciating architecture and finding new street art—people painting garbage cans, planting private flowers in the beds of publicly-owned trees, starting new urban gardens. For her going slow was always its own reward.

About four months before she died, she asked me why I was speeding along a highway to get home instead of taking surface streets. I told her it would save 2-3 minutes. "And what are you going to do with those 2-3 minutes?" I laughed. I had no answer. She often asked questions that had no easy answers. But the issue here wasn't speed so much as her need to be out and experience more of the world, the world that she was rapidly losing. Only later did I realize how important every little excursion was to her.

For Tracy, her love of slow started, like most, with the "Slow Food" Movement. Along with "Slow Travel," she quickly took up the cause in other areas: "Slow Money," "Slow Cities," "Slow Homes," "Slow Reading" and even "Slow Writing." Going slow was her lifelong habit. But she suddenly awakened to multiple rationales for what instinctively she already loved. She even blogged about it. When electronic reading came into vogue she gathered data and explained the physiological and mental virtues of holding physical books in your hands. She even bought an old typewriter and banged out a few letters to friends. But she was no Luddite. Times were changing regardless of her judgments about them. She was not one to remain fixed on past realities. She adopted Facebook and Twitter years before me. She even got an I-pad, enrolled in an instructional class, and took to using it to read the occasional essay.

The need for her to get out and experience something of the world became more pronounced before her death. She was depressed. She spent many days largely alone in our bedroom. Days that could have been filled with visits from friends and family, providing respite from the ennui that also accompanies the dying. (If you're keeping score, depression is the 4TH of Elizabeth Kubler-Ross's five stages of dying.) Partly because she didn't want to give up hope, partly because she didn't want to overly concern others, she let only a few key people know the situation was dire. Her sisters came, and a few friends. She spent many days largely playing the online game "Bejeweled." This seems an essential part of the process the dying need to separate from the living. But the few visits she got really lifted her spirits. She noticed this herself; the more she had to do the better she felt.

One of her last excursions was to the car wash with her daughter and me. Talk about slow! I love this inexpensive, locally owned business where each vehicle is impeccably hand washed. Where a dozen or more capable men take tremendous pride in the workmanship that rare employment affords. Where customer service is stretched into new territory: coffee, tea, milk, juice, bottled water, fresh fruit, granola bars...all are freely offered to waiting customers. But wait you must. We stayed there for an hour and a half.

Tracy loved every minute of it. It was a warm, sunny day. We found a plastic lawn chair for her to sit comfortably in the shade under a suspended tarp at the back of the lot with the rest of the patient. Surrounded by a ramshackle fence with weeds poking through, card tables and folding chairs...this is West Oakland, not a tourist destination. And in all sincerity she told her daughter, "Isn't it wonderful here?"

That's the kind of saint she was in her final days. Her usual preference for slow became snaillike. Nothing left to do but fully experience all that's happening exactly as it's happening. She grew absolutely attentive to everything that was around her. We'd go for walks to Lake Merritt and sit on the benches. "Look at the pelican!" Her senses were keen and she relished everything. "What a beautiful tree!" "The water is unusually clear today!" "Look at the light reflected off that building!" Similarly, every wrapper, container, and product that was brought into the house became an object of fierce scrutiny. "Is it reusable?" "Recyclable?" "Bio-degradable?" "Was it locally grown or shipped from afar?" "If I can't consume or use it can someone else?" Every food product, every book shipment, every box, plastic bag, piece of junk mail...all became grist for the mill of Right Livelihood and impermanence. One operative question trumped all other concerns. What can we do with this thing that can maximize its utility while expediting its passage on to its next most effective use?

I misjudged it all as her having gone PC. That she'd gone off the deep end and become a fanatical purist. And I don't deny that it was wearisome to have her complain that I bought tomatoes from Mexico rather than wait till Saturday to get them from the local farmers' market. She was raising the bar. Everything had to meet the standard of 100% sustainability. In fact, for the last 10 years she was continually raising the bar on our lifestyle awareness. In 2009 she couldn't wait to get rid of our 2ND car. She probably wouldn't have minded getting rid of the first one. How much more could we cut back? What was truly important? What do we need to live by?

This approach to life and lifestyle started in LA in 2007. She began saying, "let's scale down, let's scale down." I was shocked. Scale down?! I wanted to scale up! I felt like we were barely holding on to a middle-class standard and I wanted a Mulholland Drive mansion with a hot tub and swimming pool! I've always been a hot tub maven. I love swimming. I would love my own lap pool. Welcome greed! Welcome grasping! Only in retrospect do I understand that she was expressing life's highest calling by attending mindfully and compassionately to everything that crossed her path. She was embodying her love of all of things, all creatures, every precious gift that the abundant planet offers us, manifesting her deepest nature, inhabiting her greatest goodness. She was becoming a Buddha. She didn't want to pass any homeless person without recognition, providing some modicum of support. She didn't want children to pass unacknowledged and unblessed. Babies especially. She didn't want dogs or cats to go unpetted, flowers and plants to go unpruned or unwatered.

My habitual impatience inveterate, I was only dimly aware of this. But slowly, inexorably, I too was changing, becoming more patient, alert to the present. Tracy herself reflected this back to me 7-10 days before she died. She had crapped the bed. There were dribbles trailing from the bed to the toilet. I woke up as she was groggily trying to clean the sheet. She was upset with herself. I sprang up and immediately started reassuring her it was all right. I thought when someone dies this stuff is normal as normal can be. I had it handled. I *wanted* to handle it. Mostly I wanted to hold her and keep saying, "it's OK; it's OK." I ripped the blankets off and stripped the bed. I was down on my hands and knees washing the rug when I heard her say, "You have gotten so patient." I looked up to see her expression of wonder and kindness. I laughed sheepishly but I was deeply touched, both to be recognized by her and to see the truth in her statement. I *had* changed. Not because of any special effort on my part, not because I wanted to when for so long I knew I needed to, but because I was simply fulfilling what was expected. Being dutiful had begun to work a change in me. I was simply doing what was expected, what any caring and aware person would do, frankly, what any normal person *should* do. But I was extremely grateful to receive this reflection. It had been a long time coming. That said, it's also fair to say it didn't last. After she died and that profound sense of obligation left me, except for fulfilling her wishes there was little left for me to do or prove and I felt the old impatience return. Still, for one shining moment I felt extremely honored and blessed. Leave it for shit to help us realize the transcendent.

I recently ran across this relevant quote from the wonderful book *Zen Seeds* by Shundo Aoyama:

> *The Zen term kanshiketsu literally means "shit-stick..." Shit-sticks, which were used in former times for the same purpose [as toilet paper], could be washed and used any number of times. Shit-sticks become dirty to clean us. If these are not buddhas, what is? Out of gratitude for them I recognize the shit-stick as a buddha. And this makes me wonder whether, if I were given a filthy task, I would be able to tackle it with*

the same attitude that I would deal with any of the duties of abbess. Would I happily take pride in it? I would probably complain, compare it unfavorably with other work, and be tormented by a feeling of inferiority.

... In the mundane world there are countless roles and degrees of status. In the world of truth, the world of the Buddha, however, nothing is useless. Everything is equally important, irreplaceable, and precious. Nothing is inessential. If there were no toilet paper we would not get through the day. If a garbage truck did not come around once in a while, we would be in serious trouble. Getting smeared with excrement or covered with dirt is the ultimate form of buddhahood. We may think we understand this, but when it is our turn to get our hands dirty we end up complaining. (p. 91)

Three to four weeks before she died we met with the hospice spiritual counselor. He remarked on how equanimous she seemed, peaceful with a quiet joy. "I don't have time for troubles, disagreeables and pettiness," she said. "It's true. You really seem at peace and happy," he said. "I can see it in your eyes." If only we could all live this way. As if we're dying. Because, of course, we are. Each moment beckons us to awaken to its fullness and celebrate its glory. Alas, too few of us recognize our time is short. Even if our time is long, say 90 or 100 years, it's short. Eternity is long. There is only now. Tracy understood this. Certainly in the end, but throughout most of our time together, every moment mattered.

In June 2011 Tracy and I embarked on an RV adventure together. She called it the Book Tourpalooza. It began as a complete disaster. Everyone has at least one specific primal fear and Tracy's was to end up living in a trailer. I managed to make this fear real. She needed to promote her book and I needed to promote my film *Journey from Zanskar*. I thought it would be a lot of fun to buy an RV and travel together doing both. Ever since I was a kid I loved the idea of portable homes; I had long romanticized RV travel. Somehow I convinced Tracy to do it.

First, she arranged a book tour with libraries, cafes, and bookstores, getting every gig she could across a wide arc spreading north through Washington State, east to Omaha, down through and across Kansas, then back through Colorado, New Mexico, Arizona, and southern California. I played clean-up, following her bookings by setting up screenings of my film at theaters, community centers, and Buddhist groups in those same or nearby towns. We went head to head and competed with each other for an audience in Sandpoint, Idaho. But most of the time we checker boarded events effectively, and rarely had to drive more than a few hundred miles in a day's time to make a gig. The schedule also contained gaps, making it possible for us to visit many of the West's most scenic spots, like the Black Hills, where I'd never been. I thought it a perfectly splendid idea impeccably executed, at least before we left.

The trip proved almost catastrophic. Becoming trailer trash and moving all the time were in fact the top two of Tracy's primal fears. Losing control of her life was a close third. My RV fantasia fulfilled all three, a trifecta of misery. If only it were all her fault. But I had plenty of my own fears. I'm the least mechanically inclined man I know. Yet I had appointed myself 'Captain Trips' in a winking nod to Jerry Garcia and the 1960s acid tests. Ken Kesey and Neil Cassady annointed their cross-country traveling LSD bus extravaganza "Furthur." For us, given my ineptitude, often going any further at all became a challenge.

Did I mention losing control is also a primal fear of mine? It's only made worse when it comes in the form of a woman whom I'm only too happy to project the worst aspects of my mother's controlling behavior onto. If that wasn't enough, inhabiting the RV, shielded only by a thin sheet of tin, made us feel extremely vulnerable to the ever-present sounds of people, traffic, and machinery from an outside world in perpetual motion. Sleeping in a tent is easy—you give yourself over to the wild. Trying to sleep in an RV is confusing because you're neither inside nor outside. Or, more accurately, you're inside outside. I wanted to stay in National Forests, off the road in seclusion, or on deserted urban streets. Tracy felt safest in RV parks, suburban streets, and Walmart parking lots.

Tracy hated moving. She moved 13 times in the first eight years of her life—a peripatetic lifestyle well documented in her book. Every move felt like a literal uprooting. In yet another of our diametric oppositions, I feel equally at home anywhere. I lived in the same house from ages 6-17, and again from ages 30-32. What uproots me is my own desire for change. That willingness for new exploration kicks in and I ask "Where to now?" I love discovering new people, places, cultures. Then I'm happy to settle down…until I get restless again. I'm lucky that my work is exceptionally portable, and this was true even prior to the digital age.

In recent years my Wanderlust has cooled. Partly because air travel has become an experience akin to industrial chicken farming. Partly because my desire to experience the new and different has taken a backseat to my need to be of use. If travel doesn't further my work or provide a worthwhile service to the people at the other end it's of little value to me anymore. I have no interest in traveling solely as a tourist. Not at all, anywhere. Though I still yearn to hunker down in distant ports to learn again from everyday foreigners, ideally to live there for some time, unless I know my own gifts are of practical use, that there is some quid pro quo, then I'd rather abstain.

Five seconds after leaving home in the RV with Tracy, I hit a tree branch on the block where we live. Two hours later, the central valley temperature nearing 95 degrees and rising, we discovered the air conditioning didn't work. We spent the afternoon at a Ford dealership in Corning, CA getting the problem temporarily repaired but not solved. Tracy barely made her first bookstore reading in Redding, CA. Only a month later in Salina, Kansas, when it was 105F and what remained of our marriage depended on air conditioning, an intrepid mechanic effectively disassembled the entire engine to find the nest in the recesses. Turns out we had been harboring fugitive pack rats who were feeding on the hoses. By this time, though, the rats themselves had jumped ship. Maybe it was too hot for them.

Tracy's writing from the trip is characteristically better than mine so I now quote a paragraph from one of her blogs:

> *The worst possible option for RVers who actually want to sleep in their parked vehicle is a rest stop which doubles as truck weighing station just 15 yards from the Interstate outside Spokane. You can see where this is going. Let's just say that between the parking lot lights, the infernal whoosh whoosh of the Interstate, and the coming and going of 18-wheelers, neither I nor Captain Trips slept, and as so often happens when there are so many other things to blame, one of us who shall remain nameless was especially testy, blaming the other one for stealing all the covers, when a simple survey of the bed would have revealed that all the covers had, indeed, been stolen, but not by the person being blamed. If the blamer couldn't sleep, he might have taken a glance out the bleepin' window. In the interest of marital concord, plan ahead. If you don't, and end up driving and driving into the night desperate for somewhere to sleep, anywhere will be more restful than a rest stop.*

Given that Tracy had cancer the entire time I knew her, with Stage IV cancer for all of the last ten years, it's amazing how fit and active she was. She regularly did yoga at home most of that time. When we took our first road trip together to Milwaukee to visit my brother's family in the Spring of 2003 she went jogging with me around the nearby park. We often did hikes in the Sierras. Many of the physical activities I wanted to do she would take part in, even if it meant scaling back my original intentions. Until our fateful Book Tourpalooza.

Like a lot of guys, I can be extremely goal oriented when I hike. "Let's go to the summit and watch the sunset!" "Only five more miles to the waterfall!" "In three hours we should reach the trail intersection. Let's have lunch there!" "Let's find out what's over that crest...around that bend...behind those rocks...on the other side of the river..." (Pretty much everything I say on hikes has exclamation points.) Woe befall the hiker joining me who doesn't share this accomplishment zeal. Like Tracy.

Our day at Yellowstone started reasonably enough. We got on our bikes and headed a few miles down the road to the trailhead of a seldom-used path. We locked the bikes and headed in. The real problem was that the terrain and wildlife weren't interesting. No geysers, no big lakes or canyons, no mud pots, no waterfalls, few birds, few hills, no scenic views, a modest, lazy river, certainly no bears or elk. I'd chosen a completely boring trail in a spectacular park. After a few hours I got "more-itis." "Just a little further...let's get to the top of this hill...maybe when we leave the trees and get to the next meadow...let's have lunch on that hillside boulder..." On and on we went for miles. I thought there must be *something* there of interest. Tracy was exhausted. Finally back where we'd parked our bikes, she was hunched over the railing, her hair matted with dried sweat. I still remember how pale she was when she told me "that's it. I'm done. No more forced marches." I myself was almost too sore to bike to the nearby lodge where we went for drinks and rejuvenation. She was miserable. We never did long hikes together again. Thank god one of us had some sense.

Our marriage barely survived making Boise. Not knowing where we would sleep each night drove her crazy. Fortunately, Tracy flew from Boise to Indianapolis for a week to do some readings. I drove away from the airport convinced I was driving straight to a prostitute to satisfy urgent needs, assuage male pride, and get revenge. But as soon as she left the vehicle I felt tremendous relief and the urge subsided. I made friends in town, rode my bike everywhere, spent days at the library, and had a sold out screening at a wonderful indie multiplex called Flix. Thank god for just-in-time time away from each other. We certainly had problems after that but relations became somewhat easier. Our understanding of the RV deepened, our knowing of what each of us required got clearer; we grew less troubled and had more fun. We grew to love it so much that by the last month we were truly saddened to give it up. What cinched it for us were three blissfully peaceful days in an upscale RV park in the Palo Verde Valley desert in southern California. Abandoned for the summer, we had the swimming pool, tastefully landscaped grounds, and surrounding desert entirely to ourselves. The heat dried out whatever remained of our simmering discontent.

Our August 15 wedding anniversary happened along in Kansas, in the midst of our summer trials. Here's the note I wrote to Tracy that day, verbatim:

> *I'm not proud of what my part has been in the difficulties over the last few months. All the underlying issues of course are not about you. But I have yet to get a complete handle on what they are and won't know until I do some work in my I-*

group [men's support group]. Certainly continuing to speak our truth to each other about what we're feeling is good.

Please know that I still treasure you and our relationship. The difficulties we've faced are in no way a reflection of my long-standing commitment to you. I'm in this for the long haul. I appreciate you now, even more really, than the great love I shared with you on the day we married. Thank you for being committed to me and to us. Thank you for being the amazing woman you are. You're still my dream come true. I love you.

But back in July we were still near full boil in South Dakota. After a rough couple nights in the Black Hills I steered us to the Lakota Reservation in South Dakota—Pine Ridge, and to my friend Ed Young Man Afraid of His Horse. I knew approximately where his place was, off a dirt road a mile or two northwest of Kyle. But I couldn't find it. The one previous time I'd been there we arrived from the north and east. This time we came in from the south and west. All dirt roads suddenly looked the same.

How I ended up knowing Ed has a few of its own winding roads. Somehow a good portion of my adult life has been devoted to advocating for the initiation and mentorship of young people. In a sense it started when I was nine, when my father died and my uncle told me I was the man of the house. It took off with my own initiation courtesy of MKP, two weeks shy of my 40TH birthday. Then, five years later, in the midst of making *Boys to Men?* in Newark, N.J.—an elaborate statement on the problems facing teen boys—I realized I needed to make a film about solutions. That led me to research teen initiation and mentorship. Who was doing it? Where? Utilizing what methodology(s)? Those from indigenous people? Modern social inventions? Hybrids?

I found Luis Rodriguez—poet laureate of Los Angeles, candidate for governor of California, journalist and writer, change agent. In Chicago, in 1994, Luis, along with his son and other young people, helped found an organization called Youth Struggling for Survival. Those inner city Asian and Latino youngsters, many former or potential gang members, as Luis himself once was, gravitated to Frank Blazquez, also known as Tekpatzin, a trained pipecarrier and teacher in the indigenous ways of U.S. and Central American peoples. Frank poured sweat lodges in suburban Chicago and prepared the young people for Lakota style initiation in Pine Ridge. He took them to Ed's. Frank and the YSS community graciously welcomed my friend Ben and me to join them in the summer of 2006.

On his ranch, Ed embraced the youth, poured sweat lodges for them, and after further preparation, turned them loose for Vision Quest. Consistent with the old ways, the young people spent up to four days and nights in a circle about six feet in diameter, abstaining from food and water, praying for a vision to inform their lives. I experienced a truncated version of this myself and spent 12 hours in the brutalizing sun of a 100 degree day. I have lifelong respect for the young people who accomplish this rite of passage.

After the young people returned, had another sweat lodge, and ceremonially received food and water, they would talk story around the fire. Ed interpreted their experiences, helping them understand what particular expectations the ancestors might have for them. Like most true spirit guides, he did this all as a giveaway. He received only the traditional offering of tobacco. Guests chipped in on groceries and the workload, making meals together in Ed's little trailer.

Like many who carry good medicine and welcome all comers, Ed knew celebrities and became a bit of a celebrity himself in the white world. In 2011 Diane Sawyer joined Ed in the lodge and produced a 20/20 episode about his work with youth. She was so impacted by the experience that she insisted her friend Oprah Winfrey call Ed for a conversation. According to Frank, Ed also worked with Harrison Ford, Henry Winkler, and two of the surviving brothers of the Walton Walmart family. It's somehow typical for many indigenous teachers and healers that those relationships never translated into some visible forms of material support for Ed.

Center: Frank Blazquez (in the Sox shirt) and his wife Louise; background right: myself and Ben Stake; far right: Ed.

Throughout the year, Ed also poured weekly sobriety lodges for men. They would pray in the lodge for support with their addictions and other life challenges. They usually arrived with a food offering to be shared following the sweat.

Like many in Pine Ridge, Ed was not an easy man to reach. These were the days before cell phones were common, and he could be off anywhere at any particular time working the ranch. The outgoing message on his landline said he'd do his best to get back to you, but…"on Indian time." I suppose he returned calls now and then. But I learned to keep calling until I reached him. Though I don't think his laugh was recorded on the machine, I can hear it in my head now when I think about that outgoing message. He gave all that he had to give, and felt especially called to support young people. I didn't see him again until that summer of 2011.

Lost in the RV with Tracy, I pulled into the dirt front yard of somebody else's trailer home. I got out, knocked on the door and asked the young woman there if she could direct me to Ed's. I knew it was close. She said she didn't know him. I assume she was lying. It's common and understandable practice in Indian country not to tell white strangers where your neighbors are. They've only too often proven to be heralds of doom. I got back behind the wheel.

Following further enervation we finally arrived at Ed's shady culvert home, and I pulled the RV into his front yard. After giving him tobacco, soon we were sitting on lawn chairs sipping iced tea. He didn't ask how we were doing. He didn't need to. He launched into a long monologue about anger. I can't remember a word of it. But I was dumbfounded. He was addressing all the challenges we faced traveling the road together yet we hadn't spoken a word of it to him. What he had to say was deeply incisive and soothing. Though I felt shame at being seen so transparently, all my misbehaviors so lightly outed, my psyche laid bare, Tracy and I were both immediately calmed. If there were a single turning point to our summer travails that was it. What he did for me was incomparable and I'm most grateful, like a kindhearted grandfather telling me to wake up, grow up, and show up. For reaching deep into Tracy's spirit and smoothing her sense of grievance I bow in everlasting gratitude. She loved him in the first ten minutes.

I can't even remember whether we were there long enough for the weekly lodge. But given the gift we received on our arrival it probably wasn't necessary. We left there a day or two later, chastened. I never saw Ed again.

Frank sent me an email on August 6, 2014, the day Ed died. He was only 62. I was shocked. He was a big, strong man who, though certainly no health nut, was fit. Frank said Ed's grandsons went to wake him and when they couldn't, they got his brother to enter the house. It was he who determined Ed was dead, presumably in his sleep. What could have caused his death I have no idea. He smoked but not heavily. It's a mystery. Heartbreaking. Such a good man, and so young. Tracy was saddened. But we had already seen so much death that year, and with hers only two years away, she took it in stride.

The last fight Tracy and I had was, not surprisingly, about our core conflict, our mutual struggle for power and control. It took place about a month before she died, while she was in the hospital. I had been spending as much time as possible with her, mostly afternoons and evenings. We'd make laps together around the hospital floor. It was good to keep her exercised, to help her bowel move, constipation being the whole reason for her admission as a patient. She'd take my arm and we'd circle the rooms, commenting on how lonely some older patients seemed, witnessing two Code Blue episodes. This must have been the floor for the dying. We'd nod to the nurses at different stations; chat with someone going in or out a room. It was a big floor. I think our record was four laps. Of course, I always pushed the envelope by asking her to go one more than she seemed willing to. "Let's see what's around the bend!"

We'd check in with each other on the phone, through email, and texts every morning. I liked being with her physically so I could sit in on meetings with doctors. I would ask them how necessary the meds were, about alternatives, about future prospects and the end game of different scenarios. They always seemed open and accommodating of my questions and concerns. Following one such visit Tracy told me I came across as arrogant for not deferring to their expertise. This took me aback. I thought I was being respectful, a reasoned and strong advocate for her wellbeing. She perceived my questions as challenges to their professionalism and thought me presumptuous. She clearly was experiencing an unusual depth of gratitude and calm being in the hospital. She felt like she was in good hands, very well cared for.

I too appreciated the depth of concern and the quality of the care she received. But I had lots of questions about the course of her care and the multiple drugs they so readily administered. I'm not sure how this crossed a line and became arrogance and presumption. So I experienced a quandary. I wanted to be in the hospital not only to keep her company but to be her clear and consistent advocate. She seemed to be saying, "don't be." Maybe this was another part of the dying process. Maybe she was shifting wholly into gratitude. Perhaps that journey means not challenging those entrusted with her care. Under most circumstances I did my best to defer to her wants. But this seemed counter-productive. Who was going to have her back if not I?

The question simmered in me. Thursday evening June 9 it boiled over. We'd done a number of laps and I was making ready to leave. Tracy wanted to go to the bathroom before I left. She got up and started pushing her IV Pole Caddy. The nurse called out for her to watch out because it was still plugged in. Tracy unplugged it and the nurse left. When Tracy started to move again I saw that she hadn't noticed another wire on the floor in her path. I said, "Watch out!" Maybe the sharpness of my voice frightened her. But she instantly turned on me.

"You treat me like I'm a little girl who can't take care of herself. It's condescending. Stop it!"

"I tried to stop you from tripping and falling!"

"I saw the wire! I'm not blind! I'm not helpless! Stop telling me what to do!"

I hissed, "You are fucking impossible," and stormed out.

I no doubt should have recognized what was happening as simply the latest chapter in "You're not the boss of me." But I'd had it. "Fuck her. Let her fend for herself. I won't be treated like this…" Fortunately, her sister Tara was scheduled to arrive the next day. I resolved immediately not to return to the hospital. In fact, I realized I had to get out of town. I was trying to do what I could in service to her and I got shit for it. It was too much. I was no doubt also exhausted, nerves frayed, from months of caregiving. I spent the rest of the night fuming. Obviously, I was just really hurt. In less fraught circumstances a simple cry of "OUCH!" and a deep wail of pain would be sufficient. But I wanted to take her head off.

I think now that she must have needed the contretemps to finally flush her bowel. She sent me an email after I left the hospital, telling me she finally crapped for the first time in two weeks. Or maybe she called and left a voicemail. At 11:30 pm I sent this email response, subject line "shit:"

> Glad you pooped.
>
> I won't be coming in today. I don't want to be an irritant to you and I certainly don't want any more abuse from you. In fact, I'm going to leave for a few days as soon as I can figure out where I'm going. Tara and Peter can look after you. Feel free to give them all the shit you want. I'm taking a break.
>
> If you want to carry your control issues and your bad Dad projections about me to your grave that's your choice. But I don't have to subject myself to them when I'm only trying my best to look out for your wellbeing.
>
> Goodbye.

At 7:24 the next morning I received this email:

> Always the victim, never the perpetrator.

My thoughts? "I'll show you victim, bitch. I'll divorce you! You can fucking die on your own!" That's how I felt. Fortunately, I chose not to respond. Fortunately, at least one of the self-help lessons I'd learned over the years had taken hold: don't respond when you're angry. Then an hour later I got this email:

> Does it ever occur to you that something in your own behavior might have contributed to yesterday's tension?

She was good at that. Throwing whatever anger or frustration I had back in my face. All I knew was that I had to cease all communication with her and get out of town fast.

I immediately sent emails to a few friends to see if anyone within a day's drive might take me in. I was afraid if I went back to the hospital I'd slug her. By coincidence, a flyer landed in my inbox from a friend in Mt. Shasta—an announcement that he was pouring a sweat lodge on Sunday. That sounded like good medicine. I texted him and he said I should come up. By then it was about noon. I hadn't yet heard from the first friend I reached out to. I decided I couldn't wait. Sitting around at home was making me crazy. I needed to put some miles between Tracy and myself. I also wanted to be gone before Tara arrived so I didn't have to explain all this to her. I needed a caregiver vacation. Like, yesterday. I knew Tracy would be in good hands with her sister. I also thought, "Let *her* drive Tracy crazy for a while. Maybe then she'll appreciate me."

It's no overstatement to say that with every new mile away from Oakland I felt better. Man, could she push my buttons! I spent the next four days in the cool clear air of Mt. Shasta. I hiked the mountain. I went to a nearby hot springs, got sun and had a good soak. Poured my heart out to my friend Tom. Watched my beloved Warriors begin to throw away their NBA basketball season to the Cavaliers with Finals losses two and three. That didn't calm me down! For the first time in my life I watched the first two episodes of Lord of the Rings, hoping fantasy/adventure might help. I helped Tom with the lodge on Sunday where we did special prayers for Tracy.

All the while I kept checking my phone expecting a text saying "Tracy's dead. Come quick." Fortunately, all I got were messages from her sister about her late flight and logistics for entering the house. I was stuck in my righteous anger but I was also sick with anxiety. I didn't see how to resolve it and I didn't want to return without a resolution.

But I did it anyway. I timed my return to be sure Tara had left. I really didn't know what to do. Tracy was back home, in bed, when I walked in. I said hi but went about my business putting things away. I didn't hug or kiss her. We established that we were both still pissed at each other and that our walls of ice were solid. After a half hour or more of the deep freeze she asked me what my behavior meant, what my intentions toward her were. I said I seem to have no choice but to be her manservant and keep my mouth shut about what I think might constitute her proper care. I said if that's the case, if I can have no input into the care of my most beloved, then I choose to keep my emotional distance.

I realize now that this is not an admirable position. But I reasoned that it would be tough for me to remain loving and engaged and somehow give up any interest in her health and wellbeing. I couldn't wrap my head around doing both. Maybe what I missed was one more step in my own letting go. Maybe

I needed to drop my own commitment to her well being, to let her proceed to death in her own way, without my oversight. That's when she broke down, "I'm dying! I can't have you emotionally distant. I need you. I'm sorry…" She cried. We hugged. I cried. We cried together. Hearing her say I'm sorry really made a difference for me. Maybe she did it only as a last desperate measure for restoring peace. These were desperate times. But it moved me off my stuck position to hear her accept some blame. I'm a pig-headed SOB. That was the last fight we had. She was dead within four weeks.

CHAPTER 5
THE BEGINNINGS OF THE ENDINGS...

Living with cancer means that one key question consistently recurs: "Is this the beginning of the end?" Most people with cancer live through many cycles with this question. Tracy and I both did our best not to invest in thinking about beginnings and endings. We tried not to hold our breath, not to let the fear build every three months when it came time for another round of tests. We'd try not to consult the runes of our intuition, or take as evidence how Tracy had been feeling immediately prior to tests. Certainly we had many months, whole years, when results were good and Tracy motored along. But it felt like a losing battle. The mental pull toward that question is immense.

Certainly February 2006 was the beginning of the end when Tracy's cancer moved to the bones in her back. She went from Stage I diagnosis to Stage IV. Certainly August 2013 was the beginning of the end when the last of the estrogen suppression drugs stopped working and, since her radiation dosage levels had already been maximized, she had to go back on chemo. Fortunately, they were chemo *pills*, less toxic in their overall impact on the body. But the cancer had moved to her liver. Certainly October 2015 was the beginning of the end because the chemo pills had proven ineffective. The tumors in her liver were growing. Now she had to get chemo through an IV and was going to lose her hair again. January 2016 was the beginning of the end because the IV chemo drugs were not slowing the progress of the cancer, now spread to her lungs. Certainly May 6 was the beginning of the end when that second, more toxic chemo was not having discernable impact other than making Tracy nauseated and weak. She could hardly keep food down. She went off chemo altogether, and onto painkillers. Certainly that was the final beginning of the end. Or not.

On that May 6 day when we arrived in San Francisco for her appointment she broke down crying in the car. She said she didn't want to go. I just held her and waited. I was perfectly prepared to turn around and drive home. "I understand," was all I could say. It's shocking how little you can say at moments like these. In conversation after conversation "I understand" was the most I could muster. "I don't want to die," she'd cry out as I held her. Finally I just stopped saying anything. Fuck words. They're insufficient or inappropriate.

If only we could have had the penultimate conversation about ending her chemo treatments with Dr. Lopez *before* she got that final toxic dose. Then she might not have spent the first week of her brief, remaining post-chemo life feeling like shit. But he came round only after she finished the dose.

I took him aside and mentioned that I had upcoming trips planned for Colorado and the UK. "Should I cancel them?" He nodded. "She's not responding to the chemo positively in a sustained way. She was doing fine just a week ago. The test results were good. But now she's clearly in a lot of pain and the cancer is spreading again."

We returned to Tracy's side. He proceeded to have a more in-depth version of the same conversation with her. "I can't go on like this," Tracy said. Dr. Lopez nodded. "It's having no discernable positive impact. It's time to give it up. It's not making a difference and you don't have the strength to stand up to a stronger, more toxic chemo. In the best of worlds you'll gather strength, put on weight and be able in six months to try a different, stronger chemo." Not an encouraging prospect. Certainly nothing to pin hopes to. And there it was. Maybe the first, only and real beginning of the end.

"I'm in shock," Tracy said when he left. We sat together in silence and felt the enormity. I held her hand. She cried softly. I waited until she was ready. There was nowhere to go and nothing to do. On our way out, one of Tracy's favorite nurses who tended to her lovingly for many years came rushing up to us in the hall. She threw her arms around Tracy and wept. The two held each other and cried together softly, whispering final endearments. It must be immeasurably difficult for the nurses and staff in the oncology ward. They tend so ably, often for such long periods, to their beloved patients, only to see them suddenly disappear with a death sentence and, probably more often that not, no final goodbye.

And yet, that wasn't to be the final beginning of the end. Tracy continued making plans for visits well into August with friends and family. She talked about taking sick leave in the Fall. She even mentioned accompanying me to an October conference in Cancun. Two weeks later, on her final visit with Dr. Lopez, he said she might have six months. To us that felt like a huge reprieve. I let myself be lifted by the prospect.

But I was kidding myself. In my gut I knew better. She was going fast. I found myself caught between the public position I took with Tracy—"Six months!"—and the private one that I shared directly with everyone I could—"Come fast!" The big hope was that she could live to see her second grandson born in early September. He was actually born five weeks early, the end of July.... but that turned out to be three weeks after Tracy died.

Between all those beginnings of the end comes a lot of living. The phrase is truly meaningless unless it's applied equally to everything, which, again, renders it meaningless. I now use it only tongue in cheek. Certainly every breath has a beginning, middle, and end. So does, in a sense, every moment. Following the course of Tracy's cancer all these beginnings and endings, deaths and births, were real, and yet not real. If only we could live our lives knowing we die in each moment and are reborn in the next. Then maybe when real death comes it won't seem like such a shock. We'll experience it as the most natural course of things, the latest in a long series of similar dyings.

Tracy knew her dying was hard on Dr. Lopez. She came back from that final meeting with him with those very words on her lips. That was so like Tracy, to be concerned about how others who cared for her were taking the news of her dying. She was one of his shining success stories, having made it through ten years with Stage IV. They had a marvelous relationship. When she would cry he would tear up and hold her. It was abundantly clear that he truly cared for his patients. He loved to laugh. His raucous howl was audible throughout the ward. But she felt let down by him in the end because of his awkward and uninformed hand-off to palliative care. In that final goodbye, she felt uninformed and uncared for. We had little clue what the pain-killing meds he had prescribed would do. There was no warning how they would constipate her, setting into motion a series of complications that eventually led to her eight day hospital stay a month later.

> MAY 12, 2016
>
> About 2 weeks ago we were in bed together and talking about her dying. She turned to me and said, crying, "I don't know how to do this. I've never done this before." Of course I started crying and I said, "Me too. We're both virgins." This is what happens when people are totally unsupported by their culture in experiencing and facing death. And of course, no matter the preparation, we're all virgins until it's our

time. We need both. To get the cultural support we need to prepare and to recognize that ultimately we will take that journey alone.

Sitting now in her office while she's off teaching her last class... last class of the semester, last class of her college career, last class forever. That's the biggest challenge perhaps these days—being with and in every moment while also experiencing it as a moment of future—projected nostalgia. "Is this the last time ___?" That goes through my head ~20X a day. I suppose it's natural but it's essential that I don't let it get in our way.

When Tracy returned from class she began her final look around her office. She knew she was closing out her professional life. She took a few things she had immediate need for at home. But then she examined her walls full of books. Though a mere fragment of the many she had collected throughout her lifetime, there were 100s. "You can give my books to the library." She cried and I held her. "This will be my last time here," she said with a steady voice. She loved that office and she loved everything it represented about who she was in the world, how she succeeded in becoming the woman she wanted to be.

She loved libraries—arguably one of the remaining few functional institutions of our dysfunctional democracy. The place where all can come and be served, filled and made whole by the wisdom of beings. We both saw them as houses of worship. They held her, nourished her, and loved her through the remarkably even course of her life. Much as the main public library in Philadelphia held and nourished my mother through the vagabondage of her youth. Tracy wanted her books to return to libraries, to the collective, back to the agora of free thought. Her office physically connected her to the USF library. Its glorious 4TH floor view overlooked the biggest green space in the whole of campus, opposite St. Ignatius Church, with a great view of the library off to the right. She loved doing her work there. By rights she should never have had to give it up so early.

I returned there August 9 to clean it out. Though I had no desire whatsoever to do it a mere 32 days after she died, I knew Tracy would've wanted me to. I could hear her admonition in my head: "I'm dead. Let someone else use it. Office space is very hard to come by on campus. I don't need a monument to my work." I emptied out and recycled her sippy cup. I went through those books, taking the few I wanted, conscious I'd probably never take the time to read half of them, coveting them nonetheless. I tossed her toothbrush and kept her toothpaste. I took a stack of Sharpies and a 75-watt tungsten bulb that she supplanted years ago with energy efficient CFLs. Unlike Tracy, my aesthetic preference for warmer-toned light always trumps the priority to do the environmentally right thing. I took her lamp, Japanese end table, and some paintings. I also found a folder from 1999 labeled "Notes from Kate," her daughter. She added "And Erin" (her other daughter) to the label later. In it were fax cover sheets she'd sent them both concerning the memorial in Montana that summer to spread her mother's ashes. There were little notes from both her daughters, photo booth sequences of Tracy with each of them, a big Valentine's Day card from Kate, and other photos from that time. Strange how it was only from that year, that summer, that time. 1999. No other files, no other years, no other saved mementoes. Those were the last years the girls were girls. She kept that hodgepodge file for 17 years. Given the paucity of other files in that drawer I'm sure she didn't forget or misplace it. She wanted it by her side.

I closed the door and walked out. Her assistant Katie pointed out the poem on the glass she had taped under her nameplate. "Read Me," a prose excerpt from "Honeybee" by Naomi Shihab Nye.

Watch us humans
as we enter our rooms,
remove our shoes and watches,
and stretch out on the bed
with a single good book.
It's the honey of the mind time.
Lights shine through our little jars.

MAY 9

The process for a human being disengaging from life is a long and slow one. I see it showing up in lots of little ways with Tracy. Starting months ago—at least October if not much earlier—she used to sit at the kitchen table for hours on her computer looking at Facebook and Twitter, checking emails, but mostly surfing the web reading news and other articles of interest. Now she mostly plays solitaire and Bejeweled, a video game. I know she's playing it now, lying on the bed. I can hear her sniffling. I imagine it's all part of the process of letting go. The story I tell myself is that it's necessary to grieve all that is being left behind. Everyone will have their own way of coming to terms with their demise.

MAY 11

She talks about dying so readily now. It's been a somewhat sudden, but also slowly evolving process over the last 4 months or so, going back to January, starting with "I don't want to die" cries of anguish. But considering that we just decided Friday with Dr. Lopez to cease chemo—and at that time her response 15 min. later was "I'm in shock"—yet here it is only Monday and it seems she's in total acceptance. She's been making gallows humor jokes about it all yesterday. We sat down and made a list of all the things we have to do beforehand—she by far more than me. I keep saying death doesn't arrive with a Save the Date notice but now I'm wondering if that's not true. If we really listen and observe closely maybe death does arrive "on schedule." Tracy is certainly doing her own magnificent, accepting, generous part to welcome it. To have this kind of time to plan…it's just so much the opposite of what everyone exclaims when they first receive such news—"There is no time left!" Not true. There is plenty if we take it with acceptance, and don't act in denial. Grace emerges naturally if we accept what comes and make room for it.

May 15

"On one hand I want to still live a long time but on the other I want this misery to end quickly. It's pretty confusing." "I feel better when I'm busy, when I'm doing something." No doubt. She got the clippers out and shaved my head. For the last time? Telling me "When I'm gone you can get $7 haircuts at the barber college at MacArthur and Telegraph." "There're so many things to take care of. I'm afraid I'm going to forget some…" I said it's inevitable and I'll deal with them. As per usual, she doesn't want to leave me with them, to be burdened by them.

May 16

I'm so grateful for easy and peaceful days like today, with no great storms of emotion and tears. When Tracy doesn't feel too awful, and spends time in the kitchen sewing, planning her quilt, even humming and singing for periods of time. Sweet and easy. So glad.

May 28

Tracy seems to be moving inexorably to accepting euthanasia. She says she doesn't have it in her for sticking it out to the bitter end. I understand. There's some beauty and power in deciding for yourself—"enough." And in determining when that should be. I only cautioned her against making the decision based too much on what's better for everyone else, especially her family. She's afraid they won't be able to take a long, drawn-out dying process. I get that. But I think it's important the decision puts her needs first, making sure it serves her first and foremost. I don't want her to go to her grave primarily living out and through her caretaker role for others. Plus, who is she to decide what's best for her adult children and other family members? This could be an opportunity for significant growth for many of them. Not to mention a decision contrary to their own wants and needs.

The other night in bed Tracy was commenting on how she feels different strange bodily sensations. Like someone was walking on her toes. Or we were having an earthquake and the bed was vibrating. I assured her that I wasn't experiencing those things. Certainly the pot and other drugs like Dilaudid are contributors. But I also wonder if it isn't death closing in, announcing his presence, creeping around.

JUNE 1

"I will not vomit. I will not vomit. I will not vomit…." Tracy walks down the hall chanting aloud. Now she's in the bedroom coughing. Soon she'll be in the bathroom vomiting. It's painful as hell, for her of course, but for me too. And it's making me furious not to be able to do anything about it. I can see how caregivers can become abusers by turning their frustration and impotence on their beloved patients.

JUNE 16

Tracy is turning into a skeleton right before my eyes. Last night as we lay in bed talking I looked at her profile and it was like she was already dead, her skull hanging in a professor's lecture hall. I can't believe how much weight she's already lost. It's like the decomposition process can't wait until after death, it's getting a head start. The sight takes my breath away. I hope she can last another month so her family can at least all see her before she passes.

It pisses me off that Erin is not scheduled to come for another 2 weeks and Kate isn't even planning on coming. It seems like another generational failing in the making.

I pointed out to her my concern that her daughters might face half a lifetime of regret by not visiting Tracy more, or at all, before she goes. She said she'll write Kate and explain the urgency of the situation. We'll see if and how Kate responds.

JUNE 19

Tracy looks like a Holocaust survivor. I can feel all the bones in her back when I hug her. She's in the living room now watching TV. I guess that's how it goes now. When she's feeling better she watches TV in the living room. When she's not feeling well she stays in bed and plays video puzzles and naps. I keep projecting all the things that I would rather be doing when I die onto her and I need to stop. Whether it's going for a walk, sitting in the park, listening to a good book or a dharma talk, getting a massage or doing a hot tub soak, whatever sounds good to me is not necessarily, or often remotely, what she wants. I just want these last days to be meaningful and fulfilling. Maybe just being peaceful is enough.

JUNE 28

We had a date today and went to the movies to see The Lobster and had dinner. Tracy tried to pay for the movie tix but got confused and couldn't handle coming up with $17 for us. It's heartbreaking. It's not the disease; it's the drugs. She drifts in and out of consciousness all morning, mostly napping. In the movie—late aft—she dropped off a couple times for a while. I put my hand over her eyes to double-check. And now her ankles are swelling and getting yellow spots. And her eyes turned yellow. All from the jaundice—the breakdown of the liver. It's happening so fast it seems. Can she really make it another 4-5 months? It seems so unlikely. I'm glad Kate has finally decided to come July 25(?) and Erin will be here Thursday. The time is NOW! There are no tomorrows. She's so frail.

JUNE 29

She's been bringing her fingers to the sides of her mouth often in the last week. I asked her why. She said, "checking for drool." Since I didn't believe there was actually drool there—I only saw some once or twice—in recent days she took to wiping her mouth and showing me. "See. Drool!"

Now when Tracy zonks out from the drugs she has this weird habit of holding a hand to her mouth, a finger often to her lips. She'll be totally conked but frozen in that position. Her eyes rolled back in her head, her mouth open, sometimes her head tilted back, other times not. It's painful to see—it's a death mask, a prelude to the final moment. It's no doubt to check on whether she's drooling.

JULY 1

Perhaps the hardest thing of all to see go in her is mental clarity. She has such a sharp and beautiful mind. Now when I'm talking with her half the time she nods out and is gone. Increasingly while talking she'll say things that are complete non-sequiturs, coming out of her dream landscape. It's hard to know when I should engage and follow up with "what?" and ask for explanations or what to just let go.

JULY 5

Yesterday I resolved to be grateful for every day that Tracy is still alive. It started on Sunday July 3, when I left Tracy and Erin to go for a swim. Erin was lying on our bed holding Tracy's hand as she drifted in and out of consciousness. I left thinking "Tracy could die right now." That'd probably be a good way for her to go—holding her daughter's hand, having her close. So I went swimming with that thought. Of course the whole time I found myself obsessing that she was dying as I was swimming. So when I got home I was delighted to see her still alive. That's when I resolved to be truly grateful for each day she has left.

So it's good to remember that. Especially now, only 2 days later when it feels like it could happen any moment. Tracy's spent all morning sleeping. But when she wakes, as she's done the last two nights throughout, she's confused. She sits up quite suddenly, tries to get her bearings, then launches herself forward—either to the bathroom or out the door to the hallway. If she goes into the kitchen or living room she'll sit for a few minutes, confused, and then get up and go back to bed. Is this the motor of life kicking in when it still can, at random, creating movement for its own sake when discernable purpose has gone away?

She's also getting more "difficult." Refusing to take certain meds "because they taste bad." Telling me to stop asking so many questions when I ask where she's going in the night. Telling me it's too much pressure when I hold her hand, however lightly. I assume it's all part of the final stage of letting go, when even the presence of the beloved is too intrusive and the dying need to be more with the dead. This morning she asked, "Why are all the little girls in the movie?" If there are a lot of little girls there, sounds like a good movie for her to be in.

So today is now the official beginning of the end. The hospital bed is being installed in the bedroom. Gabriella was here at noon and said most likely a few days to a week. I've contacted the key relatives—all 4 women. Hopefully Erin and Kate will get here tomorrow and not wait til Thursday. She's going fast. She's been sleeping all day. When she gets up she flutters about with anxiety then lies down again and moans or sighs. She's confused. But Gabriella did get through to her about the urgency. Later Tracy said, "I'm in shock." No doubt. The poor girl's been thinking she has at least another month, maybe two. I certainly didn't want to disabuse her. And now here it is. It seems Shannon will only book her flight if she knows the exact date of her death, i.e., if she's opted for assisted suicide. Otherwise, she's waiting for word of the funeral. Sheesh. Tara's in Scotland. I sent her an email.

I'm glad I'm cried out for the moment. I've been breaking down sobbing off and on all day. How someone so vibrant and alive, albeit slowed, one day can become so near death the next is amazing. But that's literally the case between yesterday and today. I know that in time it's her beauty, vibrancy, and aliveness I'll most remember but this is tough. She looks like she aged ten years since yesterday. Literally. It's like someone just pulled the plug. I have no idea what I'm going to do with all her stuff. Hopefully her kids will take most of it.

At least now things are set for the end. The hospital bed is here, the commode, the side table…everything a person needs to die. And no sooner had I written earlier today that at least she has no breathing problems she duly reported that she does. She can't get enough air. So on the advice of the hospice nurse I gave her .25mg of oxycodone. Hopefully that'll help. I also gave her 1mg of Haldol a little before 4 hrs. but who cares?

And still there's a part of me that hopes I'll wake up tomorrow and find that it was all a dream. I'll roll over and hug Tracy, and we'll laugh together at some of the sillier things that have happened.

And now Kate and Erin are driving down, through the night, to get here by 7:30am. Finally—a sense of urgency.

July 6

Events are happening so fast I can't keep up with them. Tracy is now expected to die within the next 24-36 hours. I was trying to calm her anxiety this afternoon, telling her to relax, that all is as it should be. Her brow was furrowed and her neck muscles taut. I asked if she was in pain and she said no.

Reminds me of a brief conversation from circa 3am 2 nights ago (? They are all blending together...) When she sat up, as she would so often, and sit confused on the bed I asked what she was doing. She said, "I'm wrestling." " What are you wrestling?" I asked. "I need to fidget," is the answer I remember. Or "I'm fidgeting."

I get it. Or so I imagine. Does dying feel like resignation? All those efforts to sit up and walk into the kitchen were like an assertion to life. "I am alive and I can assert my will." Is that the very last thing to go, the last vestige of living to be surrendered to death? Or is it that I'm being too philosophical and it's really much simpler—she had nervous energy she needed to burn off. Now that I think about it, it's probably that. Tracy was always simple when I was prone to lofty pronouncements.

July 7

A beautiful soul has left this plane. Sweet, beautiful Tracy is no more.

After sitting a couple moments in wonder I thought I better wake her girls. I knocked lightly, said "your mother's gone," and they came in the room. I had my head on the metal bar by her side; I started sobbing. Not just at my grief for having lost her but at the beauty of it all.

We sat together for a while, crying. Then I got up to smudge the house. I burned a large bundle of sage, carrying it through the house, ending in the bedroom where her body lay. I smudged Tracy and the entire room. I may have been muttering prayers. I called the hospice number at Kaiser to report she died. She said Gabriella was scheduled to stop by at 7 am anyway. I told her there was no need for her to come sooner. Tracy's daughters went back to sleep. I lay down on our bed right next to Tracy's hospital bed and rested.

Gabriella was her usual prompt self and showed up at seven. I explained at the door that Tracy had died at 4:27. She gave me a hug. I showed her to the bedroom. She examined her, double-checked for a heartbeat and pulse, then sat down on the bed. I went to reawaken the girls. When I returned I noticed Gabriella had wiped away the soft foam that had formed between Tracy's lips when she died and had remained there for the subsequent few hours. I asked her about it and she confirmed having done it. "Aesthetics," I thought, and smiled. She did look better. You could see the whiteness of her teeth. A whiteness that seemed all the more remarkable in death than in life, given the yellow pallor of her skin and the shrink-wrapped sheaf of her torso.

That's when Gabriella told me about removing the body. She explained to me that legally I could take up to 72 hours before having Tracy's body removed. I was so grateful. I assumed that it had to be handled immediately following death. It gave me the opportunity to spend a final day with Tracy.

She reviewed other information for me—the legal and medical protocols of dying, disposing of the meds, arranging for pickup of the bed and wheelchair, getting further bereavement support from hospice. I asked her something about herself. She commented on how working with some of her best patients was all too brief because they often died quickly and peacefully, with relatively few complications. After a few minutes, assured that all was in hand, she hugged me and left. I knew it was likely the last time I would see her. But somehow it only occurred to me later that I was making yet another lifetime goodbye.

At some point, I gave the girls some time alone with their Mom. I asked them again if they wanted to join me in washing the body. Both said No. I filled a washbasin with warm soapy water and set about my task. Rigor mortis had already stiffened the body considerably. Rolling her from side to side was hard enough but to get to those hard-to-get areas was much more challenging. Thinking back now I wish I summoned the wisdom to sing a sacred song or two. Instead I cried the entire time and repeated over and over how much I loved her. I was able to remove her diaper. I noted with sadness how she wet herself slightly and wondered if that had been recent or some hours ago since it had been almost 20 hours since we put it on.

    I have no understanding why but I believe washing her was one of the most profound things I've done in my life. There must be a reason why so many religions insist on the practice. Obviously, sanitation and health. But aside from that? Maybe because it's the final act of devotion. I know no other possible answer. In Jewish tradition, it's considered the only act of giving/kindness that expects no gift in return. Somehow it seems the perfect bookend with wedding. In a Zen wedding like ours, we bow to each other at the altar. Marriage should be a partnership based on deep mutual respect and equality. In death, we figuratively bow to our beloved again by cleaning the body. The greatest number of photographs I have of Tracy are from our wedding. They surround me now. They too are part of our time together. They too remind me of my final opportunity to love her body.

After washing her, I remember sitting on the bed trying to meditate. It was extremely difficult. I kept wanting to throw myself on her and weep some more. Tears came and went but the pull to her body was immense. Maybe it was my desire to die too. If so, I only grew conscious of that later. This wasn't monkey mind. This was some gravitational force pulling me sideways, back to her bedside, back to gazing in wonder at her face in death, her sublime final repose.

I recently ran across this quote from "The Death of Ivan Ilyich:" "*The expression on the face said that what was necessary had been accomplished, and accomplished rightly.*" That was certainly true about Tracy. She had done all that was necessary and she did it in a good way—righteous and loving. That's why with respect and honor I share one of the photos I took within an hour following her death.

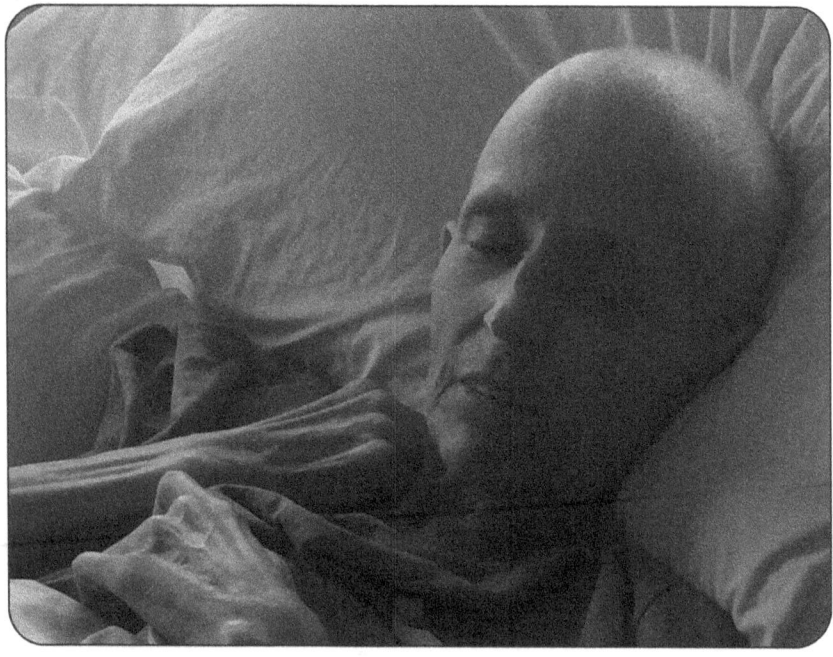

I hope Tracy would approve. She certainly stood for truth in dying. She approved anything that might help another face their own death or face the dying of a loved one. She still looks beautiful to me.

I spent much of the afternoon alone with her. I had relatively few things to tend to and with Tracy's sisters arriving the house was already filling up. I got to retreat to our bedroom for solitude and peace. To lie beside her with the quiet and the soft afternoon light was healing.

I remembered the experience of my father's death and the overwhelming sense of having nowhere of my own to be alone with my feelings. Now I felt tremendous gratitude that, finally at 60, I had a place to go, to be. I had the bedroom that we shared and I had her body beside me. I even had our master bathroom to use if I needed it so I wouldn't have to walk out to use the one in the hall where the others were. I could be fully alone with my grief. It was such a relief. Everybody always says, "Now she's at peace. Now she's no longer suffering, in pain." I didn't feel any of that. What I felt was an immediate connection back to the life we shared for so many years. A life of tranquility, peace, and ease. With her there not breathing beside me I felt safe and comforted, our relationship restored.

I braced myself when it was time for me to leave the room. But eventually I needed to be a host, tending to other people, making arrangements. Family members needed to return home and resume their lives. We set the private family viewing and memorial service for 48 hours later. If it were up to me alone I would've called the funeral home, told them to pick her up in three days, and spent the entire time there in the bedroom with her. I would've had the memorial service a week later. Life intrudes upon sorrow. I suppose it's a good thing. But it intrudes upon peace too.

In the evening the doorbell rang and two people from the funeral home arrived to retrieve the body. The lead man asked if Tracy was wearing any jewelry. I said no. He then wrote down what I told him, that the body had been washed. I gave him the Iranian gown that Tracy used in her final months as a housedress and the scarf that she elaborately wove around her head to hide her baldness. I wanted her to be dressed in them for the viewing. He wrote down "gown and scarf." I asked if they would be returned to me. He said yes. (And yet, they were not. They were burned with her in the crematorium.) When it became clear they could hardly lift the body out of the bed I offered to help. At that point, Tracy probably weighed no more than 120 pounds. They refused my help. I stupidly deferred. I regret not insisting. Welcome shadow! "Do what the authorities want!" "It's all under control!" I missed out on carrying her one last time. They barely managed to get her out of the bed in the sheet. With a piece of furniture I would've recommended sliding it down the stairs. With Tracy I preferred some dignity and finesse.

It's beyond sobering to see your beloved wrapped in a sheet and carted down the stairs, swinging from side to side and crashing to the floor. Those were literally the words I said when they finally made it out the door. "That's sobering." They were sweating and panting when they finally lugged her to the van. You'd think that funeral personnel would have a lot of experience dealing with dead bodies. You'd think they'd have finesse and skill. Apparently not.

I was haunted for some time by one of the final looks Tracy gave me. The afternoon before she died we moved her out of our bed and onto the hospital bed. Fortunately we had Gabriella's help. The night before had been one of our most challenging nights. I woke up to find Tracy passed out on the toilet, her head hanging down between her legs, urine all over the floor. I didn't know what to do. I woke her, then helped stand her up and somehow walked her back to bed. She was crying out the whole time in pain because I was squeezing her so tightly. I was terrified of dropping her. It was then I realized that the bed and her nightdress were also soaked. She was so out of it, it was hard to know what she could and couldn't do. I stood her up again, managing to get her dress over her head. I wiped her down with towels then grabbed a clean T-shirt to keep her warm. I wanted to use one of mine so it would fit loosely. Only when she collapsed back on the bed did I realize

I'd put it on inside-out. I knew I'd never be able to change the sheet with her in the bed so I put a towel down over the urine. Fortunately, it was mostly confined near the edge. I covered her up and kissed her, then set to wiping down the bathroom floor.

I should have let her sleep. But I was afraid she still had to pee. So I asked her if she needed to. Maybe she never understood my question but she said yes. So I put the commode by the bed and tried to lift her up. Again she cried out. I turned her and lowered her on to the seat. She probably never realized what was then supposed to happen. I waited a while then asked if she'd peed. She said yes. So again I lifted her, and awkwardly tried to pivot to drop her on the bed. Again she cried out. I laid her down and covered her up. I looked in the commode. It was dry.

Perhaps the vague memory of all that was in her mind the next day. Her daughters arrived about six. When the stores opened I ran out to buy adult diapers. Kate and Erin managed to get one on her and change the sheets. Gabriella arrived and said we absolutely have to get her into the hospital bed. So she made ready. When I was called back into the room Tracy was still lying uncovered on her side of the bed, naked and looking extremely vulnerable. We needed to lift her up to get her on the sheet on my side of the bed. I thought if she could simply roll over, like kids rolling down a hill, then we wouldn't have to lift her. I thought this might be easier for her and us. Then she said something like, "I don't want Frederick doing this." She knew I didn't know what I was doing. She probably recognized that I didn't realize how incapacitated she was. Maybe she simply couldn't roll over. Maybe it was the lifetime hangover from "You're not the boss of me," one final return to our last fight in the hospital. I don't know. But it stung. Clearly she didn't want me controlling the process. She didn't trust my judgment. Thank god Gabriella was there.

So we rolled the ends of the sheet and lifted her over to my side of the bed. The pressure must've hurt her because she cried out. But it wasn't too difficult. Perhaps she cried out from fear. I was perplexed. I couldn't figure out exactly what the matter was. I asked, "Are you in pain?" She shook her head, whispering no. Then I asked, "Are you feeling sad?" That's when she gave me the look. The look of unmitigated skepticism and judgment. The look that told me my question might contend for the stupidest question of all time. I was trying to problem solve. She was dying. Perhaps it *was* the stupidest question of all time.

I'm glad I have a photograph of her making a similar expression. Though her look the day she died was harsher, it was in the same vein.

I'm glad this photo is from an earlier, happier time because I will carry the memory of her penultimate look for some time with shame and regret.

The last photos of Tracy and I together are from two months before she died when I had the presence of mind to start taking pictures. Light was still pouring through her little jars. Most of our entire preceding life, in fact dating back to 1985 and my return from two years in China, I vowed to stop taking pictures. It was my typical stubbornness. "Taking pictures" was my professional work and I didn't want to "work" when I wasn't working. I also understood how photographing mediates my experience and takes me out of the aliveness of the moment. So there's no wealth of pictures of Tracy and me from our 13 years together. But I have a few. Ones often taken by others, thank god. The ones I took on May 8 are possibly the ones I prize above all others. Yes, there's poignancy. We both knew what was coming. The connection we had is tangible. Our eyes were fixed on each other. Those light beams of love that were her eyes are on high. We used it as yet another opportunity to play together. Midway through the nine photos, Tracy the Wardrobe Assistant thought better of exposing her bald head and put on her knitted cap. In later weeks she'd dispense with comme il faut and drop all remaining pretense. She didn't wear a hat or scarf to her Life Honoring Celebration. After the 9TH photo she said enough. It was making her too sad. I remember the catch in her voice asking me to stop. Here are all nine photos in the sequence they were taken.

My speech at Tracy's USF Memorial September 14, 2016:
…We talked about what I should do with her ashes after she was cremated. The last thing she wanted was to recreate the inconvenience that her family went through when her mother died, asking her family to spread her ashes from a mountaintop in Montana. Tracy was practical and didn't want to inconvenience anyone. There was also no particular outdoor location that spoke to her, however pristine and beautiful, and she'd seen a lot of stunning, dramatic vistas. She certainly loved San Francisco but never found that one specific location to call home. In retrospect, it seems like one more sad reflection of the childhood rootlessness she suffered and wrote about so searingly in her book **My Ruby Slippers.**

So I asked myself what am I going to do with my portion of her ashes? She wasn't interested in a gravestone and I wasn't interested in a grave. There's certainly a romantic in me that would've been happy to pilgrimage back to each of her 14 or more childhood homes in Colorado and Kansas and pour a bit of her ashes onto each lawn. I would've been happy to spread them in Tahoe Meadows or Incline Peak just to name two Tahoe locations where we had lovely hikes a few years ago. But no place called to me and said it has to be 'here.'

Until one morning about three weeks after she died I awoke and said to myself "Duh! USF!" "We can put them in the USF community garden that she helped found and loved to tend. We can plant a tree—ideally a fruit tree…" Tracy loved growing beautiful things that served the double purpose of feeding people. She loved urban farms and gardens. I thought a plum tree because we had one in our backyard in Oakland. She delighted in making plum jam, plum salsa, plum pudding and pie. "And we can put a bench there for reading," I thought. Though Tracy was nowhere happier than at home reading in bed, she enjoyed reading outdoors too. For this lover of all things British, she would've loved this wholly British tableau—the bench by the tree in the garden.

The plaque on the bench will say: "*For Tracy Seeley, beloved English professor, advocate of students, sower of words, young voices, and gardens, lover of life. 4/6/1957—7/7/2016.*"

So we just did a little ceremony out in the garden before this memorial. I confess I also wanted it for other reasons, partly selfish. I loved the idea of there being a place for former students and present colleagues to come and commune with Tracy's spirit. And for me too. I want that place. A place where I can come and sit and remember the beauty that was my wife. It's important to have a place, a physical place, to go and commune with the dead. Though we somehow never made the connection, no one would understand that better than Tracy—she who understood the importance of place so well.

So I think it's time to change the notion of her never having had a permanent home. It's time to say she did find a home and that home is here. USF. This was and is her home. It wasn't the places we lived together—the cities of Oakland or LA or Budapest, or even San Francisco. It wasn't the individual homes we shared—despite her great love of her place on Steiner St. or the place she shared with Pedro in the Upper Haight. I'm convinced that even if we'd finally realized her dream of buying a place in the Bay Area it wouldn't have been that place either. It had to be USF.

This was her home. The home for her love of learning. The home for her love of reading and the life of the mind. The home for her love of teaching, of growing young people into their greatest fullness. The home for her love of social engagement, for knowing that intelligence is of little use unless yoked to the service of social change, of actually doing something to make this world a better place. The home for her advocacy for the rights of workers, even worker-professors, and for women—for being treated with respect and appreciation for all the gifts each offers, even when those gifts look adversarial. The home for her love of nature—of living with the deepest awareness and respect for this fragile Mother Earth who now so needs our care. The home for her love of community, of living in communion...with colleagues and friends, yoked to the idea that life has its deepest meaning only when lived serving and being supported by those from within that communion.

We all have two families—our family of origin and our family of choice. You were her family of choice. This was the one place that held and welcomed all that Tracy had to offer. There aren't many institutions like that—that can absorb all we are as human beings. And do so gratefully. So for that I have tremendous gratitude to this place, and for all of you who were her family of choice. And yes, every family's a little dysfunctional.

So if Tracy were here today and could speak for herself I think this is what she'd say: "Thank you for giving me this home. Thank you for being my family of choice." All her life she was full of gratitude. Even in her last months. Though she absolutely did not want to die, she was tremendously grateful for all that she'd been able to do, all the friends and colleagues she'd made and loved, all the students she'd been challenged by and broken through to reach, all the administrators who sounded and shared the depth of the mission of this university...That's what she would say. Thank you, thank you, thank you!

(I originally wanted to close by reading the Merwin poem below but knew I'd never get through it without breaking down. Instead, I asked for it to be added to the printed program.)

THANKS

By W.S. Merwin
Copyright © 2005 by W.S. Merwin.
Reprinted by permission of The Wylie Agency, Inc.

Listen
with the night falling we are saying thank you
we are stopping on the bridges to bow from the railings
we are running out of the glass rooms
with our mouths full of food to look at the sky
and say thank you
we are standing by the water thanking it
standing by the windows looking out
in our directions
back from a series of hospitals back from a mugging
after funerals we are saying thank you
after the news of the dead
whether or not we knew them we are saying thank you
over telephones we are saying thank you
in doorways and in the backs of cars and in elevators
remembering wars and the police at the door
and the beatings on stairs we are saying thank you
in the banks we are saying thank you
in the faces of the officials and the rich
and of all who will never change
we go on saying thank you thank you

with the animals dying around us
taking our feelings we are saying thank you
with the forests falling faster than the minutes
of our lives we are saying thank you
with the words going out like cells of a brain
with the cities growing over us
we are saying thank you faster and faster
with nobody listening we are saying thank you
thank you we are saying and waving
dark though it is

CHAPTER 6

FREDERICK MARX
OCT. 31, 1955—?

About three months before she died, Tracy asked me to please not die before her. I was shocked that she felt it necessary to ask. Supporting her in dying had become the central purpose of my life. So I said something lame like "of course not sweetheart." I literally didn't know how else to constellate my life. What else was it for? I had nothing else to keep me occupied. I canceled all my travel, including a two month long trip to the UK that my assistant and I had worked hard to set up, planned for the end of May. That plan also called for Tracy to join me with her family in Scotland for two weeks starting July 4. Once I cleared my calendar I was looking at months of largely blank pages. But based on past experience she had good reason to fear.

I have a historic problem with suicidal ideation. Knowing that my life had value in supporting Tracy in dying helped allay that ideation. I became extremely guarded toward preserving my own life. I became exceptionally careful any time I went anywhere to perform the least meaningful task. I drove slower. I didn't run as many red lights on my bike. I didn't flip off drivers. I had somebody I loved who needed me to help her die.

Schooled in death in different ways by my parents, suicide has been my default solution for most problems. The theme from MASH—"Suicide is Painless"—is a song I sing regularly because I enjoy its black humor. But I also sing it when suicidal ideation arises. It's become a productive means of mocking myself, of shifting out of my funk. The only half-hearted attempt I ever made in that direction was when I was 18. Feeling unloved, I swallowed a few barbiturates, enough to make a puppy nap after a good run, and tearfully called my ex-girlfriend, who was the reason for my despair. I wanted her to know how much I was hurting…the aloneness, the fear of perpetual aloneness. I wanted her to hurt. I wanted her to care.

That is the point, isn't it? Not for all certainly, but for many…"I'll show them! They'll really suffer when I'm gone!" To make others hurt as much as they've hurt you. To let people know, in no uncertain terms, how hurt you are, to make them realize, only too late, that they really care for you. "If only I'd reached out to him! Told him I really love him." The ways and means of fantasies are many. That's why they call it *ideation*. It's the *idea* of dying that's so satisfying. Just think of the pain it will cause others!

I've always taken the suicides of others especially hard, be they celebrities or common folk, whether personal acquaintances or not. I took Robin Williams' and David Foster Wallace's suicides hard. Two men with such extraordinary talent and wisdom. I get that they both struggled for some time with mental health issues. They truly suffered and, unlike me, were in terrible pain. Is that enough of a trump card to take the final step?

This obsession is part of why I'm making my film *Veterans Journey Home*. My heart goes out to all the Vets committing suicide—an estimated 22 each day. It's an epidemic. But the deeper truth is I always take it personally. How could so many others commit suicide and I not have the nerve? What made them cross the finish line that I have been unable to cross? What was the final straw? Why not continue with the pain, the heartache, for another day, at least another moment? And the shadow question: Why should they be so lucky to finally pull the trigger and not me? My craziness abounds. I can turn *not* committing suicide into an example of my own victimization! I'm a victim of my own aversion!

I always wonder about these things. Call it prurient voyeurism. What was their final decision-making process like? Is there something there I could learn from? Something to avoid? How might their final moments be similar to or different from my own?

I realized sometime back in the mid-90s that the moment I would most likely act on the urge to kill myself would be in a fit of pique, in frustration over something small, like being unable to untie a knot on my shoe or breaking a handle on my suitcase or knocking a glass vase to the floor or, like what happened yesterday, forgetting about a pot of boiling potatoes until I could smell them burning. Whatever the proximate cause, the internal dialogue is much the same: "You fuck up! You can't do anything right. You'll never do anything right. You are a miserable excuse for a human being. You don't deserve to live. Do yourself and the world a favor by getting out of the way. Make room for someone who's not a complete failure." This monologue has its variations but remains much the same, and has so from the time of my childhood.

Of course it's the hangover from my father's judgments of me. I can remember how he would take me to get haircuts that he knew I hated. Unfashionable crewcuts that made me look ridiculous. He laughed the whole time, mocking my suffering. My mother acknowledged all this in later years, saying, "I never understood why he would do that." Of course, knowing the source of one's demons does little to mitigate against their arrival or mediate against the suffering they cause. At 60, it's long past time for me to blame my father. But as everything about my life with Tracy taught me, the hardest pieces to let go are the deepest parts of ourselves.

Knowing better, I now recognize that self-hating story as *one* of the stories of my life. But the story gets so loud and convincing at times it's hard to hear or remember another. When coupled with the instantaneousness of the bellowing in the wake of some "disaster" it can feel like an irresistible force. I imagine that in the aftermath of some failure or mishap, in the fury of that momentary self-judgment, I could easily just grab a knife and slit my own throat. Tripping over a shoelace, being unable to screw in a light bulb, setting off a smoke alarm…the more quotidian the cause the more likely the extreme outrage. "How could I be so stupid?! I am such a fuck-up!" The great challenge of my life is to live long enough to die a natural death, from declining health and a failing body, not to end it in an irate moment of self-vexation. I tell myself my mother made it to 87, so can I.

My friend Gigi commonly and laughingly refers to her demons as "the Dark Institute." Though I have never succeeded in getting her to explain exactly what she means by that, I assume it's a similarly bellicose psychic place she goes to when things get bad. I immediately appointed myself an honorary member.

Fortunately, I know what to do when things get dire. Get me to a Nunnery. I've learned from experience that when I'm depressed and feeling suicidal there's one thing that will always cure me—a meditation retreat. It works every time. There's nothing like sitting in silence for 5-10 days to re-right the mental gyroscope. I've never left a meditation retreat less than balanced and equanimous, extremely grateful for my life, if not outrightly joyful. Junpo, my Zen teacher and friend, said something very wise to me after one retreat. "You probably need at least one of these every year to stay balanced." I believe it's partly why he gave me the Zen name Simha. He told me it's a Sanskrit name meaning Vigilant Lion. I have to be vigilant if I'm to remain even keeled, and, yes, alive. The interwebs however—using the made-up word Tracy enjoyed—say something different. They say it means Powerful One or Powerful Lion. The bigshot side of me prefers that. But the wise part of me knows that "vigilant" carries my real marching orders. I have to remain vigilant against my own mental habits.

I went through a rough patch in 2013-2014 when I did everything but remain vigilant. In quick succession my friend and mentor Harold Ramis died, my mother died, then three of my most beloved teachers and life role models died, including Don Jones, Ed Young Man Afraid of his Horses, and Pete Seeger. Phillip Seymour Hoffman joined Robin Williams and David Foster Wallace in the brilliant dead artists gallery. I missed and mourned them all.

But that wasn't the problem. Some of those deaths were expected. I believed I was good with death. I could handle death. The problem was how these deaths reflected my own life back to me. It made me review the things I had set out to do in my early 20s. I had not come close to realizing those professional goals. Though I was absolutely mum about it well into my 30s, I fully expected that by the time I reached 60 I would be a well-supported Hollywood filmmaker, like, say, Woody Allen, directing a film a year. I also envisioned, by way of "giving back" and planning sensibly for retirement, that I would become a tenured faculty member at a major university. By the objective and measurable standards of those goals I failed.

I wrestled with the reality of that judgment. I was depressed. I knew it was time to make new goals for my life and let the old ones go. But I couldn't. Through my Buddhist practice, my Rites of Passage work, my men's work, the strong relationship I forged with Tracy, I had been successful in ways I never could have envisioned in my youth. On the personal level, I succeeded in making myself into the man I always wanted to be. On the professional level, I even succeeded in garnering recognition and many prestigious awards, including Academy and Emmy Award nominations. But I couldn't comprehend how through talent and force of will I hadn't been able to become gainfully employed as a Hollywood filmmaker. During the winter of 2013-14, I became suicidal.

For quite some years, I had accumulated a sense of betrayal in terms of my dreams, my calling. I had discovered the joys of filmmaking all the way back in my teens. By the time I was 23 I knew that to be my life's work. Nothing else gave me the fulfillment, the meaning, the sense of purpose that filmmaking did. I couldn't understand how years of sacrifice and hard work making excellent films had not led to the promised land of on-going institutional support. This conundrum drove me crazy. "Why have I failed? Where did I go wrong? What decisions should I have made differently?" I wanted to have a good agent and manager, bringing me great scripts and well funded documentary projects. I failed. I wanted to be in the Directors Guild of America. I failed. I wanted to be in the Academy. I failed. I wanted to partner with production companies, studios, and broadcasters. I failed. How could this happen? If this was meant as my life's calling, my vocation, why didn't more success and support appear? I thought the Hero's Journey was supposed to lead me to being crowned professionally as a successful director/writer working regularly.

That thinking usually led straight into the sewer of hurt and regret over partnering with Steve James to make *Hoop Dreams,* released in 1994. Certainly every time I look at his life since then, I'm struck by how he's lived out almost every opportunity that "rightfully" should have been mine. Somehow he inherited *my* karma. I speak German; I've lived in Germany; I know the country, the history and the culture. He made a film in Berlin about a German boxer. I've lived in China; I know the country, the history and the culture; I speak some Mandarin. He made a film about Chinese immigrants. He even made a documentary about Roger Ebert that should've been "mine" to make. Roger got the film reviewing bug partly from my dad who founded the Foreign Cinema Club at the University of Illinois Champaign-Urbana. I myself wrote film reviews at the same Daily Illini newspaper where Roger got his start as a writer and editor.

John Pierson, the man who, along with Roger Ebert and Gene Siskel, helped launch *Hoop Dreams* into the stratosphere, chose Steve as his go to guy to make a documentary about him and his family when they opened a movie theater in Fiji. But I was the person who first met John. I knew his work, and, recognizing how he could be supportive of our film's release, I was the one who reached out to him and brought him into our *Hoop Dreams* family.

Somehow Steve appears to be living the life I thought was meant for me. Some of it has to do with the fact that by prior agreement Steve got the sole directing credit on the film. I call myself an uncredited co-director. Certainly that missing credit accounts for much of it. But all of it? Even Peter Gilbert, our other Hoops partner, somehow inherited some of "my" karma. He got to direct a feature film that one of my college friends wrote—a woman I stayed with during my many visits to LA in the wake of *Hoop Dreams* success, but who somehow never turned to me to direct her film. The film got savage reviews. I haven't seen it. But I will say immodestly I would have made a better one.

I try to take whatever solace I can in a quote I spotted from Wes Jackson of the Land Institute in Kansas, one of Tracy's friends and heroes. I use it as an email tagline: "We are not called to success but obedience to our vision."

The thing is, I still have a lot of films I'd like to make. Knowing my shadows—impatience with process, which comes across as arrogance toward public institutions, corporations, and their public faces, e.g., service workers and clerks, even colleagues; my unwillingness to schmooze and grease the levers of influence; my loathing of self-promotion, salesmanship and marketing...none of these understandings has meant a goddamn thing in helping me to succeed in spite of them. I try to partner with and hire people who can cover my deficiencies but it never seems to make a significant difference. Knowing those shadows also didn't help me ease into acceptance of my failures. With rapidly changing technology and the wild transformations wrought by the Internet, the bottom dropped out of independent film financing and distribution, making it largely untenable for me to continue. The model I grew up with in the 70s and labored under for 30 years—make excellent work and they will come—ceased to exist by 2010.

So, for those years of 2013-14, I was obsessed with suicidal thoughts. If I wasn't accomplishing my goals then it was best to end it all. If I wasn't able to do what I felt certain I'd been put on the planet to do then it was time to give up. Tracy and I discussed it many times. She was sickened by my depression but was largely helpless to assist. She did make valuable suggestions. One was to return to making short, experimental and personal essay films like I did in the 80s. She also encouraged me to do more service work, bringing me in closer proximity to people who could benefit from my contributions, who might connect with me emotionally and provide inspiration. Certainly through my non-profit company Warrior Films I did a lot of useful work to launch a movement around youth rites of passage and mentorship. She also encouraged my writing, whether screenplays, blogs, or essays. Writing is in fact somewhat becoming my default mode of artistic production since the regularity of filmmaking has subsided.

I also had long conversations with mentors and friends about options. I knew the old vision for my life needed to die but I couldn't see my way forward to a new one. I needed a rite of passage. In lieu of one, I accepted that the purpose of my life had become supporting Tracy. Perhaps I never made this explicitly clear to her. No doubt thankfully since "I'm living for you baby" is likely of specious comfort to anyone with any sense. But supporting her through her entire dying process became my central raison d'etre.

There were times when she knew it was safe to kid me about being down. "What's a matter, Bunky? Life got ya down?" she would say in a cartoon voice. Or maybe it was Eddie Lawrence she was imitating? That's one of the greatest gifts we can give to those we love—learning how and when to gently turn the mirror around so they can see themselves, only now with Groucho glasses, a bulbous nose, and pasted-on moustache. It was certainly one of the treasures she gave me. She kidded me about my neuroses and got me laughing. I tried hard to reciprocate, especially when I triggered her. I'd mock her and say, "You're not the boss of me!" and squinch my face. On good days I could get her to laugh.

She asked me once how I envisioned killing myself. "A gun." That's how I always pictured it. Much quicker and easier than most other methods. Messy, yes. But the ease and finality are hard to beat. That's why I'll never buy a gun. I know too well I would be its first and only victim. For me to bring one into the house would be even stupider than using it on myself later. Most victims of gun violence are their owners' immediate families. All too often gun owners leave their weapons accessible to children. As a gun owner myself I'd be another in a long line of idiots. I can see the headline: "Marx Shoots Inner Child."

Tracy expressed surprise at my answer. She always imagined I would use insulin. She gave me more credit for intelligence than I deserved. When I told her I never considered that, she was astonished.

It was, in fact, a great idea. Inject too much, slip into a coma, and be gone. Simple. Relatively painless. No mess. The most obvious approach simply hadn't occurred to me. Shows you another feature of ideation—it's not creative thought. It's repetitive patterns of highly uncreative thought. Having the needle stuck in the groove of an old Black Sabbath LP; you get the same three minor chords over and over again. I thanked her for giving me the idea. She didn't appreciate my black humor and was summarily unthrilled with herself.

CHAPTER 7
THE AFTERMATH

AFTER TRACY DIED, almost every day, often many times a day, I was asked, "How are you?" I decided I had to stop answering. The question is well meant but meaningless. It's impossible to answer partly because I never know the time frame in which it's meant. "In this second? In this minute? For the last hour? Today? Since I last saw you?" Every answer could be different and the answers grow in complexity with ever-widening time frames.

There's no way to reference "How are you?" to my overall well-being. It's an irrelevance. As a broad answer, what usually comes to mind is the title of a fine book by Nick Flynn. It's *Another Bullshit Night in Suck City* thank you very much. I used that phrase for a few weeks to greet myself every morning. Tracy recommended that book to me. She always brought wonderful books to my attention, especially ones with themes she knew I appreciated—coming of age, father/son relationships, suicide.

The question is complicated further by the way people look at me, with long faces and searching eyes. It seems they half expect me to throw myself on the floor screaming. Exactly whose need am I filling when I answer their question? Another broad answer for me typically is "Fine." Not because it's an automatic response, like it is for most people, but because in that moment I usually am fine. I'm with company, usually people I like and enjoy. I like people in general. Why wouldn't I be fine? Then there's the play of my own narcissistic wounding. In that moment I'm being seen and appreciated. Why wouldn't I be happy? The challenge for me is when I'm alone. So when asked how I was doing I took to saying, "I can't answer that."

One friend wrote me three weeks after Tracy died. He was very concerned about me because I'm usually so diligent about responding to emails. He knew Tracy had died yet he practically insisted on hearing back from me. So I responded to ease his concern. That's what close proximity to death and dying does for you—it forces you to become a caretaker of others completely removed from the process. A different person, a colleague of Tracy's who was kind enough to bring us food in the days leading up to her death made it clear to us that Tracy's dying had a terrible impact on her. "You don't know how this is affecting *me!*" she exclaimed. Tracy and I had a few bittersweet laughs over that.

How do I deal with her loss? I drink every evening to kill the pain. That's when it's worst, the evening. The time of day when Tracy and I would emerge from respective offices, come together for a meal, and commiserate. We'd laugh at ourselves for being old fogies and take our meals in front of the TV to watch Colbert, a Warriors game, or a movie. We'd sit on the couch and hold hands. Or she'd snuggle into me and fall asleep on my shoulder. Sitting now in front of the TV is the time I feel most bereft. The time when I most want to jump out of my skin and crawl through slaughterhouse pens to destroy the human feeling within. Drinking somewhat deadens the pain. At least it will send me off to bed early. If I can get to bed then I can make it. 11:00, 10:00, 9:30...once it turns 8:00 I feel "OK, I can go to bed now." It matters less these days how early I get there just so I get there. Thank god I can usually fall asleep right away. Fortunately, I don't cry before sleeping much anymore. I don't like to. It makes the pillow soggy.

Sometimes it also feels melodramatic. Actually, I don't feel the sadness and the need to cry as much as the need to get unconscious. Quickly. In sleep there is no loss, no fear, no dying, no loneliness, no sorrow. Just egoless drifting. Like enlightenment.

Within days of her dying I decided I should just get on with it and start to live the dissolute life. Every night for a while I would make sure to have that extra glass of wine or a second beer. I bought a bottle of gin and enjoyed regular gin and tonics for the first time in 25 years. I felt inexplicably horny all the time and masturbated too much. I figured I'd eventually graduate to contracting prostitutes. I would become a full-fledged sex addict. I thought that would be the most direct and fulfilling path to dissolution. That and watching sports all the time. I figured if I want to become a bum and throw my life away these are the ways to do it. My other two near addictions were not going to cut it. Sleeping helped, even intermittently. But I was already doing 8-9 hours/day over a ten-hour span in bed, and taking naps. How much more could I do? It was boring. I couldn't keep myself in bed any longer. My other weakness, food, was never really an option because I already act out about as much as I can stand—eating cake and pie and ice cream and chocolate every time it's put in front of me. Wolfing down plates of spaghetti and heaping up mashed potatoes. It makes me sick. Literally. I can't eat any more.

You really can't kill yourself directly and easily with diabetes. You die slowly and painfully over time by losing one bodily function after another, amputating feet and legs, getting neuropathy and going blind, until finally kidney failure or heart attack take you. No thank you. I could do it in increments, committing slow suicide over a long period, but not go whole hog and try to do it fast. There had to be a better way to live the dissolute life. I was determined to try. Sex and alcohol seemed like the best bets.

Turns out I was as much a failure at failing as I was at succeeding. I failed at degeneracy. I couldn't keep up the pace. It was too demanding. I was getting exhausted and the alcohol, working well to deaden the emotional pain in the evening, was making me feel like shit the next day. I couldn't stick with the program. Who knew that becoming dissolute took more vigor than I had? If I were going to dissipate my life I was going to have to work harder.

But not much harder. Sex addiction still presents a clear and present danger. Though I have no lovers and have yet to reach out to prostitutes or even try online sex, sex thoughts are the ones that most easily hijack my attention and imagination. The temptation of sex is the bait that most easily pulls me out of the present moment, disrupts my best intentions, and leads me astray. One of many distractions that Mara—the force of illusion in the Buddhist pantheon—used to try to move the Buddha from his seat of pending enlightenment was sex, in the form of dozens of seductive maidens. Given his prior life as a prince in a splendid palace, where his every wish was perpetually accommodated, it might've been unfairly easy for him to resist. He was no doubt surrounded by the temptation of gorgeous, seductive women every day, along with his beautiful wife, well before he set out on the road to enlightenment. Me, I've got to keep my eye on that one. As long as I can keep my hands where they belong, limited to the upper half of my body, I am fine. Woe to me when they venture south.

So I go to bed early and wake up early. 4am, 5am…Sometimes I can refuse the call of consciousness for another hour or two and drift back to sleep. But most days I can't stand it any longer. I drag my ass out of bed by seven and repeat the journey. ANOTHER BULLSHIT NIGHT IN SUCK CITY. Maybe what's saved me is ADD. Repetitive behavior bores me. Addiction would be excruciating. The insipidness of it all would drive me out of my mind.

Did thoughts of killing myself surface with extra force after she died? Yes and no. The first two months were filled with grief partly at the unwelcome recognition that *I* was still alive. I didn't want to be; it's true. I didn't see any reason to continue living. And in a strict sense, there *was* no reason. Tracy was the #1 priority in my life. I existed mainly to love and assist her. Now that job was done. I couldn't envision a life without her. It took me 47 years to find her. Soul mates don't come traipsing along. Outside of sexual fancies, I had no interest in other women. Certainly not as long term partners.

But I was not overwhelmed by suicidal ideation. I was too grief-stricken. Pondering killing myself would've required too much effort. I was tired, possibly exhausted, but too present to what was needed in each moment to know what to do longterm. To want to kill myself would have meant engaging some of my critical faculties, some sharpness and clarity. I didn't have it. I was barely moving, suspended in a stew of hurt. I brewed in that soup for at least three months.

I still had too many practical problems to tend to. Like what to do with her meds. Between the methadone, dilaudid, morphine, oxycodone, codeine, Zofran, Reglan, Haldol, Lorazepam, and others forgotten, I could have opened a nice little pharmacy. I could have made a small fortune selling them on the streets of Oakland. Most tempting for me however, was keeping them, using the drugs myself as painkillers. That's the problem though…the pain. How to define the pain? After your beloved dies pretty much everything qualifies as pain. Though I had in mind keeping them to manage physical pain, or perhaps using them on long airline flights, in the back of my mind I knew they'd be too dangerous to keep. Like guns, I'd use them on myself. The temptation would be ever present; it'd be all too easy to take myself out. Getting rid of them was a smart decision. Still, there have been a few times, like those cross-country flights, that I've regretted throwing them all out.

Finding my way through her death, through my grief, perversely started giving me a reason to live. How can I make it through *this*? How *does* one survive the loss of one's soul mate? How *does* one find the will to go on when none seems present? It was my new job, something that could keep me occupied. I became a human lab rat in my own experiment. I didn't know how I could make it through but I was curious to see if endurance was possible. No prospect in life has filled me as much and as regularly as the search for meaning. I have an abiding taste for inquiry into the human experience. In the wake of her loss, no other question came forward as forcefully. "Is there a meaning to my life now? If so, what?" I can become relentless at seeking answers to dark questions of the human psyche. Even if there are none.

A few days after she died, I felt someone or something spooning me from behind as I lay in bed. It was freaky. There I was asleep when I had the unmistakable sensation of a presence lying down beside me and holding me. I felt pressure against my back. I heard the subtle creak on the mattress from the force of weight; even the bed seemed to give way and I felt a depression form from the mass.

I sat up frightened. Of course, I like to think it was Tracy. But it's only after the fact that I can reflect and wonder. Perhaps it *was* she? "Relax and let her hug you. It's my beloved come to say goodbye." Those are not ingrained reflexes. All my reflexes say "What the fuck?!" Not the reaction you usually find in stories of great romance.

And so it was a couple nights later, also in bed, also asleep, when I had the unmistakable impression of someone placing a hand on my thigh. That really spooked me. I sat bolt upright, terrified, kicking, as if I was being attacked. At first I thought it was our cat Beanie but she was out of the room. I've never lived a life of abiding belief in the otherworldly.

People like me must make things difficult for the dead. We skeptics must try their patience. How to convey love and affection when your beloved goes into a panic every time you try? Signs that you might send from the beyond like a truck driving past with your name emblazoned on it or a woman carrying a huge bouquet of Tracy's favorite sunflowers—both of which happened in the first few days following her death—are seen as happenstance. That's how I saw them. Lovely happenstance. Near physical contact like hugs are interpreted as something worse, something terrifying.

Communicating with the dead is not a talent I seem to have. I tried reading Rudolph Steiner's book *The Dead Are With Us*. He seems to take it as a given that everyone can interact with the dead. The bulk of the book seems more about how to do that and what to say. But after 50 pages of very heady writing where he doesn't mention how he knows it to be true I gave up. Since I live in California I guess it's expected that it should somehow be easy, that communicating with the dead is a given. Steiner seems to think so. But lately it angers me. The altar I have for Tracy in the bedroom is my place to talk with her. There was a period of time when I just felt resentful, when I resisted saying good morning or good night, which was commonplace for me in the first month after she died. I felt like I was getting nothing in return. So I did it begrudgingly for a while, then not at all. Of course, not doing it makes me feel guilty too. Like I'm deserting her, not to mention being childish. Damned if I do, damned if I don't. Nowadays I'm back to doing it occasionally, when I feel like it, and when I observe monthly ceremonies on the anniversary of her death.

About three weeks after she died I had a bad nighttime hypoglycemic episode. I was so confused that I thought it wasn't hypoglycemia at all. I thought it was something like a heart attack and that I was dying. I thought I should wake up my houseguest and ask him to call 911. By reflex I managed to test my blood glucose level. It was 31. Any level below 35 puts you at risk for coma. The level of sugar in the blood is too low for the brain to function properly. Another feature of hypoglycemia is becoming drenched in sweat within seconds. In my confusion I thought I can't or shouldn't eat glucose tabs, which I always have on hand in the bathroom. Or maybe I was out of them? I had no recollection of taking a potentially high dose of insulin in the evening. At times like this in the past I woke Tracy and she helped me sort my confusion. I was terrified. I knew I was alone and had to solve it myself. "Think, think," I kept saying. Then I remembered taking some insulin not long before bed and felt grateful that I could rationalize my way to the real source of the problem. That made the solution clear. Sweat pouring off my skin, I stumbled into the kitchen where I quickly made and downed a glass of water mixed with sugar. Fortunately within five minutes or so my panic subsided. I wiped up the pool of water at my feet, returned to our bedroom to towel off and went back to bed.

That episode notwithstanding, my diabetes has not been dramatically affected by the strain of her death. Maybe because I work out daily. That's pretty much all I can motivate to do. Exercise and the hot tub help keep my mind clear of the need to actually do something substantial. I can relax into getting nothing done. Emotional stress tends to raise blood sugar levels but regular exercise helps keep them in check.

Tracy really understood my disease and worked hard with me to combat it. If I were driving erratically she'd ask me if I had low blood sugar. If I seemed confused or unnecessarily giddy she'd ask then too. The first few years together when I took long periods of time to recover from hypoglycemic episodes at night she'd always get up and ask me if I was alright or needed anything. It became a running gag between us that when I felt unusually playful or ingenious she'd ask me the same question. I do get playful and easily amused when my blood sugar's low. I also think that I can be deeply inspired and especially insightful at those times. (For the record, as I write this, I do NOT have low blood sugar.)

So when she died I realized I not only lost my beloved partner, my confidante and catalyst, my counsel, my companion in silliness, my occasional lover, my raison d'etre – I lost a caretaker too. There was that little boy part of me that knew he'd lost a mother figure. All the things she used to do for me were suddenly voided. Though the man in me cried the greatest number of tears by far, that little boy cried his share too.

Now I have to rely on friends for everything. When I leave home and it seems my house sitter may be using my credit cards fraudulently I have no choice but to ask a friend to stop by the house to make sure the furniture is still there and the car hasn't been sold. Same when it comes to looking after my cat. Beanie gets lonely if she doesn't have company so I need to arrange for someone to look in on her every few days.

I feel like I'm imposing on my friends, that asking them is a presumption. I feel guilty. I know that's what friends are for. But when you get used to relying on your wife for everything it's humbling to start asking your friends all the time for favors.

In fact, losing your beloved is the greatest test of friendship I know. Who reaches out to you? How? With a card or letter? Sending flowers? A text? On Facebook? Tweeting? Are their words perfunctory or do they dig for something deeper? Do they offer you anything practical? Better yet, do they just show up, drinks in hand, saying I'm going to make you dinner and get you drunk? Do they keep coming back or are they one and done? Unless they've been through it themselves most people have no clue how to support someone in this position. Is that reason enough to let them off the hook? Has the heart become so mediated that no one even knows what a true human impulse is anymore, much less how to act on it? I know who my real friends are by how my heart reacts to what they do and say. In the wake of Tracy's death, even though all were well-intentioned, some moved me by what they said and did, some left me cold, feeling perfunctory, and some were sweet and tepid.

> *"The man, who, being really on the Way, falls upon hard times in the world will not, as a consequence, turn to that friend who offers him refuge and comfort and encourages his old self to survive. Rather, he will seek out someone who will faithfully and inexorably help him to risk himself, so that he may endure the suffering and pass courageously through it. Only to the extent that man exposes himself over and over again to annihilation, can that which is indestructible arise within him. In this lies the dignity of daring."* (I ran across this quote shared by Jack Kornfield in a recent blog post. The quote is from "Zen Master Karlfried Graf Dürckheim.")

Who's assisting my old self in dying? Who's challenging me to risk myself and pass courageously through it? There aren't many. A few come to mind: Fugen certainly, and Diana Sterling, my friend and colleague, who donated her coaching services to help me work through what the rest of my life might be about. Anyone else? Junpo perhaps. When I tell people I no longer answer the question "How are you?" I should also paraphrase the quote above so they can assist me in dying to what needs to die and being reborn to what desperately needs birthing.

One Buddhist teacher says we go to the cushion to die. As in, meditation is a practice form of death. Certainly it's death to the ego, death to that willful sense of self that says, "This is a waste of time. I have better things to do. What's the point?" The point is to master the mind rather than let the mind master us. A famous Tibetan teacher, following his first visit to the United States, was asked his impression of the people. "Lost in thought," he replied. This is arguably the greatest problem that exists in the world today. People believe the thoughts in their heads are worthwhile and true. What a mistake! There may be irrefutable logic to what passes through my mind but logic alone never generates truth or wisdom. Wisdom demands that I recognize there is no everlasting discernable "self" that I need to protect or hold on to. There *is* nothing to hold on to! That is truth. What we conceive of as ourselves is a series of stories constructed over time, mental projections.

Take it from me. I cling to the stories of wounding, of hurt, of loss in my life as if to a lifesaver in a raging sea. Like my stories about *Hoop Dreams* and all my subsequent challenges and failures. Unfortunately, the lifesaver is around my neck and it's choking me. If I'm willing to let it go perhaps I can learn what must be learned for survival, which is to float. Only floating will keep me on top of the waves. And breathing. Only taking conscious, measured breaths will keep me from panicking, keep me alive. No one and nothing is coming to rescue me, or any of us. I believe that we all have to learn to float.

If I've learned one great thing in my life it's to trust little of what passes through my mind. Half the time it's not even factually correct. The rest of the time there's nothing worth doing about it even if it is. If somebody wants to be rude or hurtful in some way they're going to do it and there's nothing I can do. Say "ouch" and, if need be, resolve to stay away from them in the future. But I do my best to not construct a story to live by out of it. This is where bigotry comes from, how isms are born, how victimization gets nourished. "Women will always betray you." "Men don't know how to feel." "Black people are _____." "Russians are _____." "Rich people are _____." "Once burned, twice shy," is a perfectly fine rule of thumb. But I do my best not to extrapolate from one situation to another, forming gross generalizations. Each situation is unique. Just like people.

I have to remind myself of these fundamental truths with great regularity. That's partly why I do our Hollow Bones Zen service every morning, reciting these words: *...I rely upon selfless awareness. I do not rely upon concepts of self and other that appear. I do not depend upon beliefs, sensations, and emotions that arise and fall away. Meditative awareness, clear intention, acting wisely, compassionately, and skillfully are this practice. I rely upon this only. I rely upon this ceaselessly...* To rely upon anything else is to risk drowning from a lifesaver wrapped around my neck. *Just float.*

At the end of Tracy's small memorial service for family and friends, my dear friend Fugen, who to that point had masterfully MC'd the entire ceremony, chose to speak about what may be in store for me. He asked the rhetorical question: "Why should Tracy die and not Frederick?" For me, this was a big mistake. We were there to mourn Tracy. Not to look for silver linings in her passing, e.g., perhaps I had more unfinished business on the planet to conduct than she did. Nobody was there to hear that she might've died for very good reasons before me. My judgment was and is that she likely would have made a much greater positive contribution to the planet than me.

Who's to say when someone's life mission is fulfilled? It's tempting to argue backwards that because they died their lives were complete. That smacks of the fatalistic. I really don't believe that some people have greater destinies than others. We're all here to maximize potential. Some are given shorter times, yes. Some, most, are handed tremendous socio-economic hurdles. But except for unearned privilege and "fate"—admittedly, no small factors—there's little to account for why some people live longer than others and make more lasting contributions. Given that lack of account I find it difficult to accept that "this was her time..." even though it certainly was her fate to be genetically predisposed to breast cancer.

This is a familiar argument that the bereaved typically have with "the gods." Why her? Why now? To me it all seems pretty random. And the perspective of perfect hindsight does a huge disservice to the dead who, almost invariably, do not want to die. Certainly Tracy didn't.

Anyone who says anything other than "life isn't fair" in response to those searing "Why her? Why now?" questions are themselves being unfair. Life *is* unfair. Painfully so. That's all I could bring myself to say to those who themselves were grieving Tracy's death. The moment anyone reaches for deeper explanations, whether arrived at through religion, culture, or philosophy, they do a disservice to those grieving.

Let the grieving grieve. Let each of us do it in our own way, in our own time. Offering explanations of any kind—"oh, she's in a better place; you'll meet her again when you die;" much less "the angels have taken her home," or "now she sits with God" or "now she's passing through the bardo for 49 days," or "hopefully she'll be reborn in a better body," even something as relatively benign as "at least now she's not in pain; she's at peace"...all of it is presumptive as far as I'm concerned. You don't have to be Christian to wonder if after someone dies they're not in some way still in pain, perhaps even tormented. Tibetan Buddhists believe that people can pass through hell realms during their voyage through the bardo to the next life. I personally don't believe any of those things. But so what? Belief systems are of no use to the grieving unless they themselves subscribe to the same set. And even then it can be dicey because death often causes survivors to question their beliefs, even their entire worldview. Based on my experience, if you as a friend or family member of the grieving don't know what that belief system is (or lack thereof), it's better not to say anything.

I'm not sure why but many of the pictures I took of Tracy in her final two months were of her sleeping. There was always something so sweet and vulnerable about her at those times. In fact, in previous years I would often sit by her side and marvel at the beauty of her sleeping. With her guard down, completely defenseless, she was exquisitely precious to me.

But now I look at those pictures and wonder if I wasn't somehow practicing for her death. The poses are remarkably similar. I've lost the sense of beauty and wonder I had when I took them. They feel morbid now. I ask myself how I could be so stupid to capture her unconscious when what I wish for are more expressions of her aliveness and vitality. I recognize now, in a way that maybe I couldn't have quite given words to as a child, that death changes the meaning of everything.

I loved the smell of my Dad's pipes. I loved the times he roughhoused with me. Even the time he threw me off his shoulders on to the bed when I bounced so hard I landed on the floor and cracked my skull. That scar clearly visible on my now shaved head is my closest connection to him. You might call it my "Dad tattoo." But I don't smoke so I never took his pipes or pipe rack. I want mementoes to be of practical use, so my ongoing life is integrated functionally with those I choose to remember. When my mother finally cleaned out his clothes 20 years after he died, the only item I took was his Hawaiian shirt, which he wore for their yearly Hawaiian themed party. I loved that shirt and wore it regularly until it became tatters. The only items from my mother I remember taking when I helped her move from her home of almost 50 years was a small spatula and a large mug. I think of her every time I drink tea and flip eggs.

Since Tracy died, it's been a tremendous solace to look at pictures from our wedding and from the run of days that followed. I put the entire folder of them on my default setting for my computer screen saver. Now I spend many happy minutes watching them float by. (*Just float!*) For some, I can't recall when and where they were taken. But each photo of Tracy—shining and alive, her skin glowing, eyes sparkling and happy—fills me with thankfulness. It's a profound and needed reminder of the many joyous days. And my god, what a beauty she was. I always knew she was stunning but to rediscover it again in these photos, after the six-month long collision with end stage cancer that totaled her body, is to fall in love all over again. She literally takes my breath away.

If that won't restore a man to health nothing will! It is no doubt strange to stare blankly at your unmoving computer hoping that soon the screen saver will kick in and your life will be redeemed. But that's how I spent part of my days in the first few months of her passing, meditating on photographs of her.

I now wear Tracy's wedding ring around my neck. She lost so much weight in her final months that she grew fearful of it falling off her finger and losing it. So I fashioned a leather necklace for her to hang it on. She only wore it a few days. I found it on her nightstand after she died, along with her sippy cup, IDs and credit cards, I-pad, laptop, cards and letters from well-wishers, and books. And then I put it on. Following my nervous hands, I've taken to putting different fingers through it during uneasy social interactions. When I feel the need to be close to her I also kiss it or hold it to my cheek. I kiss it when it unexpectedly drops to my lips during a down dog in yoga class. I can't imagine ever taking it off. It remains to be seen when and if I'll take my own ring off.

Even little notes from Tracy that I find around the house I feel loath to toss. One delight I experienced in July was turning to Sept. 8 in my datebook and finding a sticky note from her saying Nick Cave was playing with his band that night at the Shattuck. I couldn't bring myself to toss it, even after the date came and went. Such are the peculiarities of mourning.

Then as luck would have it, two days later an article in the Guardian caught my eye. Amanda Palmer wrote a review of the Nick Cave film *One More Time with Feeling*—a documentary about the making of his album *Skeleton Tree*. The album, though not originally begun as such, details some of Cave's process working through the sudden death of his 15-year-old son the year before. She wrote:

> Art reminds us. That our plans are meaningless. That help is not on the way. That our children can die in our lifetimes.

> *But I have to say, though his song subject is (as usual) darker than dark, Nick Cave acts here not as a harbinger of doom but of the lightest, noblest message an artist can deliver to us: that the choice to make art is, indeed, an act of blistering revenge against the nonsensical, cold unfairness of this world. Tragedy strikes. We can close down, or we can keep working on finding a frame in which to house all of this confusion. A black frame, or a white one... any frame at all. We have a choice.*

Yes, we have a choice. Mine is reflected in this writing. I didn't set out to write a book, much less make art. I set out to do everything in my power to put down every single memory of Tracy I possibly could. A fool's errand but one that brought me comfort. I was in a panic. The fingers of my beloved had just gone cold in my hand. I had nothing and no one to hold on to. It was not designed as an exercise in healing, in working through my grief, much less as a work that I might someday share with others. But I recognize that instinct Amanda Palmer identifies. It's in fact the instinct that has animated all the work I've ever created—how can I get these feelings out of my body? Living with them is causing me entirely too much pain and consternation. It's a form of exorcism. The only other alternative that I see is self-annihilation. Instead, I get to work on *"an act of blistering revenge against the nonsensical, cold unfairness of this world."*

Maybe that's why anyone creates. Some urgent call to resist the inescapable coming of change, the inevitable arrival of decay and death. It's a song we sing to ourselves to ease the pain, to shout back the forces of darkness, to let it be known we were here, however briefly, however insignificantly. Beethoven's "Ode to Joy," Picasso's Guernica, Swan Lake... all veritable fuck yous to the eye of god, to let it be known we once drew breath and walked with care and wonder on this place.

A case in point arrived in the mail a few weeks after Tracy died. Someone sent me the graphic novel *The Night Bookmobile*. Anonymously. No card, no note. I assume it was a friend of Tracy's. But since the book takes place in Chicago, set very close to where I once lived, I wonder. Still, it's a book Tracy not only would've loved, she would've wept over. It's a poignant story about a woman discovering a mysterious bookmobile that seems to house only the books she herself has read in her lifetime. I was in tears long before I finished. Initially I was crying because I knew how much Tracy would've loved it. She would never get to read it.

I wonder at what point do tears for Tracy become tears of my own? When do the things I know Tracy would've loved become the things I myself love? Does that point ever come? We weren't alike in all our tastes. Does alchemy occur and the gold that was within her become the gold within me? I pray for that.

Tracy and I talked about euthanasia months before her situation turned dire. I told her I would support that choice if she ever decided that was best. We were lucky. They passed a California law legalizing it in the last election prior to her death. Previously, we had discussed possibly traveling to Oregon, where it was already legal, for her to die in the home of one of her daughters. When she was in the hospital I ran across an article in the local paper about a doctor in Berkeley who was promoting euthanasia support services. I cut it out and put it on the dining room table where she liked to sit and work. But we never discussed it. I don't know if she even read it. When she returned from the hospital following her grueling bowel-clearing exercise we were already receiving hospice care. She was going so fast that euthanasia became moot. Still, I admired her for once considering it and I would have supported it as a typically brave choice if she decided it was what she wanted.

I didn't fully realize it then but part of me was still imagining there were different ways she might have died more easily, less painfully, more meaningfully. I was doing all this conscious processing of her death, meanwhile my unconscious life was doing its own work.

Six weeks after she died I had my first dream with Tracy in it. Nothing earth-shattering, but nonetheless sweet. We were in some run-down house together, maybe out in the country. There was a hard storm outside. But the house was sturdy and warm. She was doing something in the kitchen. I came up behind her and put my arms around her and squeezed her close. I kissed her neck. I loved hugging her from behind. I could wrap one arm around her breasts, the other around her belly, and have unimpeded access to the back of her neck. She said, "I took a look at your writing [meaning this]. It's good." She particularly referenced the part about "Steve and Jerry." I had no clue what this meant, perhaps Steve James? But Jerry? Maybe it wasn't Jerry but some other name.

I came away from the experience with a warm embrace of this process—doing my daily writing to keep her close and insure that all the rich memories of our life together are not forgotten.

But memories are a two way street. They're also driving me mad. Not for what they're telling me but for what they're not. I find that I barely remember many details. I remember we spent a weekend in Monterey, maybe in 2011. We took in a movie, went to the aquarium, walked along the beach, took a whale watching boat trip, ate some Mexican food… So what? I can't remember what we talked about, whether I held Tracy's hand when we walked the shore, whether we made love, whether she even liked the room, what made her happy, sad, or indifferent the entire time we were there. I can't even remember the film we saw, which is rare for me. Did I kiss her on the cheek at times when I felt especial appreciation? Most likely I kissed her hand a few times because that is my standard practice while walking. I'd occasionally pull her hand to my mouth, then place her flat palm against my cheek. But on that trip? Who knows?

What no one tells you about the death of a beloved partner is that it erases *your* life. The entirety of your time together is gone as if it never happened. Sure, for parts of it there are other participants. But your primary verification is gone. Your collaborator and confidante has been nullified. The many hours and days, weeks and months that you were largely alone together are obliterated. They exist no more because there is no other to corroborate their existence. You will never wholly retrieve them, sort them, embellish them, edit them, repurpose them, relive and re-delight in them. They might as well not have happened. I suppose it's different if you have children. They not only can testify to the shared experiences you once had they are co-creative in making them. You have reliable witnesses.

But I never wanted to have children. I equated children with all that is commonplace in "bourgeois" life: marriage, mortgage, consumerism, climbing the social ladder, suburbs...That life held no interest for me, long before I identified myself as an artist. Some parents have called me "selfish" and, spending my lifetime pursuing meaning and fulfillment, maybe I am. I did question that decision at various points in time, on rare occasions thinking, "Now may be the chance." I even had fantasies about having five girls so I could raise and coach my own girls' basketball team. But long before I was conscious of it, deep in my own darkness, I knew I would likely replicate the worst behavior of my father—belittling and neglecting my children. I didn't want to do that. I also didn't seek ego satisfactions in personal heirs, but in personal achievements. Yet now that Tracy's gone, at 60, I recognize I have little to live for. My work no longer provides the primary satisfaction it once did. If I had had kids I realize that serving them now might bring its own fulfillment and help allay suicidal ideation. They could have provided a whole new family of memories.

My personal memories with Tracy? Sure, I have them. But doing it all yourself is the very definition of solipsism. They're an echo chamber. They're less tangible than reflections of clouds on water, occasional gusts of wind. I have no choice but to drift in an ocean of "he said, he said…" floating in sometimes complex, occasionally contradictory mind dialogue realms, straining for land, for facts, at least for a countervailing subjectivity. What I really seek from memory, some of it sensory—the burn of hot sand, the gurgle of a fresh water stream, the cool of a shade tree, a sky filled with birds—is no longer available. What is available is hazy and insufficient and the horizon is hard to distinguish from the water's surface. *Just float?!* In circumstances like these I'd rather drown.

I spend days pining for my long-term memory storage to disgorge details that no longer exist in those brain cells. The digital information was somehow never properly written and no complete record of the event was ever recorded. What I long for are movies. 24 frames per second of our recorded history together that can be mined for documentary gold—that momentary look in her eye, a noteworthy offhand comment, a sudden smirk or grimace, an urgent demand to pause and rest. It's well established that minds are unreliable retainers of memory. Validation of the existence of our life together, my sole and final means of authentication, is itself suspect. A double whammy.

Death is the slow unraveling of every tie you've had, everything you've built together, every referent you've co-created, every urge to connect. As for the ongoing present, what would

Tracy have made of New Yorker's profile on Margaret Atwood? What would she have made of the stat in Harpers that only 22 states now teach cursive handwriting in school? Is this simply the way of things, that we no longer need to learn cursive because of computers? Or is there something inherently of value to learning that skill? Especially in the potential future wake of environmental, economic and social collapse? She would have had much to offer on the subject that I can't begin to conceive. I no longer have a deeply trusted, patient and abiding life partner to share all comments and observations about life's passing parade. I don't have her to share my confidences. There is nothing more precious than that. That deep sense of home in another person. Gone.

CHAPTER 8
DRINK TRACY LIKE WATER

June 13, 2016

Had a telling dream last night...I was in NYC in a giant public square. There were churches and preachers on all sides, giving sermons. I looked in a few churches and I saw crowded groups of homeless people being fed and/or bedding down for the night (while upright). But I felt gratitude that they were cared for. On the plaza I felt overwhelmed by the different preachers, all telling me what to do. I needed to get out of there but it meant maneuvering my way through many different, mostly older people. It also meant jumping off a ledge to get back to street level. Most places were too far to jump but I finally found a drop that wasn't too great.

Then I was in a cab with all my stuff heading home. But I didn't know where home was. The first place we pulled up wasn't it. I was also worried that I didn't have enough money for the fare. But as time wore on the more I checked my pockets the more cash kept coming out til I realized I had more than enough. Still, I was anxious. When we arrived at a 2ND neighborhood I was looking for markers that were recognizable. I didn't see any until we pulled opposite the last shop on the block—a key maker. That I recognized so I knew I was in the right place.

I tried to get all my bags together but fumbled and was nervous. My money was all wadded up and disorganized. But even though I never

> saw or recognized my place, much less went inside, at least I was home.

I had that dream 24 days before Tracy died. But it was only three months later, when working on this book, that I realized the broad significance of it, pointing the way toward a life beyond Tracy, beyond the marketplace of preachers and the elderly telling me how to do it, pointing to the money that would sustain me, to the keys that could bring me to a new site, to that home which is not so much a place as a state of mind.

Now, as I write this, Tracy was in my dream again this morning. Not much there… She walked past me on her way to a drinking fountain. She seemed so happy and at ease. I don't remember her face as much as the back of her body there at the fountain. When she first passed I didn't even realize it was she. Then I did and said, "Hey, you're dead." Then I realized I must be dreaming. But I wasn't dreaming! She was still there in front of me. Then I thought, "Wait. Are you nuts?" Then I woke up.

When I turned to this document to record that dream this is the first thing I saw:

I took great solace in that. Later that day, Fugen counseled me on how to analyze dreams. He learned these from his MKP mentor (and my role model) Don Jones who in turn learned them from philosopher/psychologist and fellow MKP member Robert Moore.

- Phase 1: ID Key words: Word associate with each word or idea.

- Phase 2: Pay attention to the last 48-72 hours. What significant events occurred in waking life? What stands out? List them…

- Phase 3: Connect the dots. If this dream was really meant to help inform my waking life, what key messages am I getting here? The beginning events of the dream identify the issue or problem or key insight or challenge, the middle parts identify what I'm still in process with, and the end parts point to how I can resolve it. The point is to treat each dream as a gift from beyond and allow it to inform me.

- Phase 4: Honor the dream. In hopes it will bring more similar dreams. Or thank it because you received the insight. Celebrate the dream. Sometimes when you perform the honoring is when the insight comes. It will just come. Put the "aha" in your title so you don't need to remember all the details. The title becomes sufficient to remember everything necessary.

I'll now follow the process with this particular dream…

- Phase 1: ID Key words:
  - "Tracy"…love, devotion, connection, surrender, knowing, service
  - "fountain"…eternal, youth, beauty, nourishment, sustenance, life, vitality, goodness,
  - "water"…life, eternity, sustenance,
  - "are you nuts"…rationality, skepticism, doubt, faith,

unknowing, devotion,
- Phase 2: Pay attention to the last 48-72 hours. What significant events occurred in waking life? What stands out? List them...
  - Doing ceremony yesterday to honor Tracy. It's been 2 months (exactly 9 weeks) since she died. I bought fresh sunflowers to put on her altar, and put fresh fruit there the day before.
  - Suicide Prevention Day. Sept. 10 (tomorrow) is the official day. This subject has come up a lot lately, initially through MKP but mostly connecting back to our *Veterans Journey Home* project.
  - Tracy's upcoming memorial at USF on Sept. 14. I've been working on my speech and the plans for the planting of the tree in her honor, etc.
- Phase 3: Connect the dots. If this dream was really meant to help inform my waking life, what key messages am I getting here? Beginning events of dream ID issue or problem or key insight or challenge, middle parts are what am I still in process with, end parts are how do I resolve it? Treat dream as a gift from beyond and allow it to inform me.
  - Tracy is still in my life. I've been struggling mightily with that. How to KNOW that she's still with me? That's something I SO long for but my rational mind may preclude me from accepting what's possible. Certainly through dream we can be together. Perhaps too through my ongoing celebration and honoring of her life through ceremony—regular prayers at the altar, continuing to talk to her.
  - I'm still in process with "seeing" her—seeing her face, looking into her eyes, really feeling her bodily, wanting to merge souls. She didn't stop as she walked past and I barely recognized it was she until she had

her back to me... She also seemed shorter.
- ○ Suicide is the central challenge of my life. That's no secret. Maybe following her to the fountain to drink will bring "eternal youth," keeping me alive.
- ○ Maybe moving past hyper-rationality and eternal skepticism will also keep me both alive and connected to her, to her goodness and wisdom. I have to be willing to be nuts, to be crazy, or at least willing to appear that way to others. Similar to the key life dream I had in Fall 1983 in China when I recognized I was a "freak" and that "freaks" were my people and where I belonged as an artist.
- Phase 4: Honor the dream. Put the "aha" in your title so you don't need to remember all the details. The title of the dream becomes sufficient to remember everything necessary.
  - ○ Drink Tracy Like Water.

When Tracy died I turned to the redwoods to hold my grief, though the discovery was a surprise at first. I found myself walking in Oakland's Redwood Regional Park with my brother and sister-in-law four days after she died. When we dropped down into the canyon's low-lying redwood stand I knew I needed the support of those elders. I wrapped my arms around one and wailed. It was completely instinctive. There was some vital necessity for me to have the support of a living thing 1,000 or more years old, life that had seen it all, the comings and goings of entire civilizations, including, soon, ours, that filled me with gratitude. I knew that whatever I had to release, to discharge, was going to be completely held, contained with absolute undemanding equanimity. "Grandfather, please hold my grief. I need your support," I sputtered. Those ancestors did not fail. They can hold it all.

Since then I haven't missed an opportunity. Two weeks later in Muir Woods with my sister I did the same, spending 15 minutes holding on to, weeping with, and talking to a majestic redwood off the beaten path. I brought home a baby branch to place on Tracy's altar.

It was Buddhism that supported me through the loss of my girlfriend in 1988. I came home one day after work to find her standing on the porch with her bags. She said, "I'm leaving you." Then she got into a waiting car and was gone. The shock of her disappearance was immense. She had given me no prior indication that she was thinking of leaving. We had hard times for sure, but not unusually so for any couple starting out. Her leaving dynamited the dam that held back all the grief of my father's equally sudden, equally inexplicable loss, 23 years earlier. I cried every day for a year.

A few days after she left a new friend asked me if I'd ever wanted to practice Buddhism. Had I?! It had been my unconscious desire since I was a teen. Those guides, and other books about Eastern philosophy, provided productive means for me to think about all the big questions, including my father's death.

But in 1988 I didn't want philosophy. I was tired of my intellect, of trying to think my way through emotional challenges. I wanted something to *do*; I wanted relief from the pain. So I threw myself into practice. I deeply appreciated the care and concern Soka Gakkai International (SGI) members had for my well-being and growth. I chanted the Lotus and Heart Sutras every day and aimed at strengthening my "life condition." It worked. I grew in confidence and ease. What I most appreciated was the diversity in both the small and large group gatherings. My small group met in a 3RD floor walk-up down some narrow alleys in Manhattan's Chinatown. My chanting mates were about 15 elderly Chinese women, few of whom spoke English. I was usually the lone white male joined occasionally by a few Latino or black men. The citywide meetings were even more impressive. 500 or more people would gather near Union Square once or twice a month. These, and subsequent SGI events in Chicago, were the most multi-cultural gatherings I ever experienced anywhere. Half the room was black folks, nearly 20% were Latino, 20% Asian, and maybe 10% white. Most were low income. I thought any spiritual practice that can bring this diverse group together is one that I want to be part of. I missed that diversity in later years when I first took to practicing Vipassana and Zen in California, where I found the overwhelming majority of practitioners to be higher income whites.

I met Junpo Denis Kelly, the man who became my Rinzai Zen teacher, in January 2000 while standing in line for dinner at the ManKind Project conference in Glen Ivy, CA. We compared notes on Buddhist teachings. He explained how he wanted to build the Hollow Bones lay order into the graduate school for MKP, to get men already trained in emotional awareness to move beyond that into "emptiness," into non-attachment, into the non-dual—the frame of mind that recognizes no separation between things, no distinctions or differences, "the one."

I loved the idea of practicing Buddhism with my MKP brothers. In the prior three years, I had already found myself invariably talking to MKP men about practicing meditation and to male meditators about joining MKP. In May that year, I sat the second ever Hollow Bones retreat in Providence, RI, shaved my head, bought robes, and started down the Zen path. But I proceeded slowly and haphazardly, as invariably following each retreat I would eventually get spellbound and revert to my old neurotic patterns of behavior and thought. That on again off again pattern continued for 15 years.

Following my 8TH Hollow Bones retreat, six months before Tracy died, I left Sonoma Mountain Zen Center feeling more on fire than usual. I finally had enough of myself. I wanted a divorce from my neuroses, cute as they may have been all these years as pets. I resolved to do whatever it takes to wake up. First step was to lay plans to be ordained, which I resolved to do one year later. If anyone had told me even five years earlier that I'd seek ordination as a Zen priest I would have laughed. Though I'd been a reasonably devout Buddhist practitioner for most of those 30 years, I was not predisposed to taking on titles and joining hierarchies. SGI was the first organization I ever joined. MKP was the second. Hollow Bones may be the third and last.

At the age of 60, I couldn't help but remember how my mother graduated with her Divinity Master's at 70 but never was ordained. My own pathway was easier than hers. In the wake of my retreat, I committed to a daily practice of Hollow Bones' five training elements. I took to getting up early every morning to do the morning service (Element #1: Philosophical Reorientation) and meditation (Element #2: Insight). I continued exercising as I normally would (Element #3: Physical embodiment) but made sure to do it every single day, even if that meant taking an 11pm walk. Element #4, Sacred Stewardship can involve many things, from conscious home management to grander service for the planet. For me it mostly meant providing regular service to my wife—cooking, cleaning, errands. Finally, I worked Element #5, Emotional Koans[5]—supporting Tracy through her death and surmounting the subsequent grief.

Zen practice is strong and demanding. Our Hollow Bones practice period is 108 straight days. My first stretch was January through April. Then, after Tracy died, I did another stint through the Fall. I fulfilled each element for a minimum 20 minutes each day. Fugen had me record exactly what I did for each element, partly so I could hold myself accountable for missing anything, partly to have the record serve as a model for others. Probably half my entries under "Sacred Stewardship" include "petting the cat." For one day's "Physical Embodiment" practice I put "walking through airports." Under "Emotional Koan," many days "writing and crying" are the only activities listed. Much later, entries like "being with beautiful women" and "dating schmating!" appear.

So I go to the cushion to practice death. To practice being with the discomfort or pain that arises, staying present to all the thoughts that emerge: "This is wrong...Get me some drugs; I'll never make it through this...My teacher doesn't understand me...The meditation master is a sadistic bastard." The practice is simple but it is not easy. Occasionally my thoughts appear to offer some wisdom, something that needs to be acted upon. Most of the time they don't. They need to be "heard" and just as quickly forgotten. If I practice this witnessing presence regularly then when the time comes to really die I hope I'll be well rehearsed. I'll be able to sustain living my life most fully until I live it no more. I'll continue to apply the enduring logic that hopefully has guided my life to that point, i.e., "What is life trying to teach me in this moment? What do I most need to learn right now?" Most likely that lesson will look something like "let go." "Let go of the need to take care of others. Let go of the fear. Let go of the need to change something. Let go of the capacity to walk. Let go of the shame of not being able to go to the bathroom by yourself. Let go of the need to get up. Let go of the need to speak. Let go of the need

---

5. Koans are nonsensical or paradoxical questions used in traditional Zen practice to freeze or stop the thinking mind, like "What is the sound of one hand clapping?" "What did your face look like before your mother was born?" "Emotional koans" are mystery statements we self-create to learn what drives us unconsciously and emotionally, so we can bring it into full awareness to cease emotional reactivity. My emotional koan was nothing more or less than Tracy's death.

to hold on to this love you have for your precious ones." And finally, "let go the clinging to life…"

These are the successive layers I saw Tracy shed in her own way. One after the other, peeling the many skins that grip this mortal frame. None of them are easy. All of them are necessary if we're to die consciously, if we're privileged to die methodically, over time. Some attachments take days or weeks to let go. If we're lucky we have the gift of time to cry 1,000 tears, to roll one particular loss over and over in our minds, to baste it like a bird until it's ready to eat. I am convinced that this is what Tracy was doing during her many hours alone in the bedroom. Other losses, especially near the end, must come quickly. "I can't get up and pee." "I can no longer turn over." "Now, I've lost my ability to eat…"

I always wanted to sit a Hollow Bones retreat with Tracy. In the first few years it wasn't possible because we only allowed men. Later, when gender balance became the norm, the timing usually conflicted with her teaching schedule. Finally, in her last few years, she didn't have the strength. So when I left the retreat in 2016 it was my dream that Tracy would at least attend my ordination ceremony the following year. I know how proud she would have been. Just to have her in the room, to share that one small but significant Hollow Bones ritual would have been a great joy for me. But weeks before her dying it became clear she'd never make it to January. And Junpo had yet to agree that I was even ready, that I should in fact be ordained. I discussed this with Fugen. I told him how it broke my heart that she wouldn't survive to witness my ceremony. Ever the wizard, he listened carefully, then called me back three days later. "I have a solution. I want to come to your house tomorrow and share it with you both."

It was Monday morning. She was lying on the couch. I brought out chairs for Fugen and I to sit opposite her. "I have some news I want to share," he began. "I want you to know that Junpo and I discussed your situation. He said, 'Please let Tracy know that Frederick will be ordained in January. Without a doubt.' Rest easy that Frederick is in good hands and will proceed well supported on his path." She wept softly. "He's been so diligent, getting up every morning at 4 or 5 to meditate," she answered. I cried too. I was relieved to know it was actually going to happen. I was overjoyed that Tracy got to hear the news before she died, three days later.

Perhaps even more than she fretted about her daughters and sisters, Tracy worried about my welfare. How was I going to manage without her? She rightly feared that I would become suicidal. I had the bad sense to mention this in our meeting with our hospice spiritual counselor a month before she died. I told him I feared that when she went I would want to go too. And for the first few weeks, that's pretty much what I felt. Tracy knew from prior depressions that when facing huge disappointment and loss I occasionally dissolved into a puddle, sapped of the will to go on. Thus, she was especially encouraged to see my re-dedication to practice. She saw how the Zen form held and supported my wellbeing. I believe it was a great relief to her that I would be ordained and continue on the path to waking up. No self-pity! No backsliding!

About a month before she died, I had asked Tracy if she would be willing to assist my work from the other side. No one knew better than she the challenges I faced and price I paid for them. She didn't hesitate and told me she would. (This was weeks before I learned that she already committed to helping from *this* side, i.e., directing some of her retirement funds to my company.) The support that has since materialized for my work in the last year from strange quarters I attribute happily, with no assurance whatsoever, to her.

But with complete assurance, I can say that after she was gone, a different strange and beautiful thing happened in a slow, inexorable way. It seemed wherever I looked around at the lives of others they too had lost their beloveds. One of the first I encountered by chance was an old friend from Chicago. By happenstance I ran across her name on Facebook. A talented filmmaker and a sharp wit, she seemed the perfect person to reach out to after not being in touch for 15 years. We had dated each other briefly when I was in graduate school. Her husband Mark was a fine man who I knew dimly from my undergraduate days at another university. No sooner had we reconnected than she told me he died one year ago in a sudden and somewhat horrible fashion—coming in for a routine angiogram he suffered a stroke. Once recovered, doctors noticed his distended stomach. 11 days of tests later they diagnosed Stage IV stomach cancer. Eight days later he was dead. He was only 57 and left her with two teenage children. I was heart struck. For her, for him, for their kids…We resumed an irregular phone friendship and compared our coping mechanisms.

Later, I met another old filmmaking friend in NY. She too had lost her exceptional husband, age 55, to suicide. He too had left her with two children aged 11 and 13, along with a mountain of unresolved debt and shaky business transactions. Like Mark from Chicago, David was a good, big-hearted, smart, and generous man. Learning of these fine men's deaths, both of them preceding Tracy's, pierced my heart. My eyes water still, thinking of them. In some inexplicable way, the universe seemed to be bringing me shared approaches toward my own grief.

One of the first in this nearly contemporaneous series of deaths was my old friend Lee Petrie. I hadn't been close to her and her husband since our college days in Champaign. But I always found her a truly remarkable woman and was stunned when I discovered, again through happenstance, that she was dying. It was May, two months before Tracy died. From the scraps of information I got it wasn't clear to me that she was going fast. Though I had my hands full supporting Tracy, I regret that I didn't summon the time and attention to send her a loving note of farewell. She deserved it. As do all beings.

In the months prior to Tracy dying a number of celebrities also suddenly died, including David Bowie and Prince. Though we never directly discussed how these deaths affected her personally, I hope Tracy was able to feel in some way that she wasn't alone facing the end. It's unexceptional to note that you're going to die and that everyone dies. But I liked to imagine that these deaths were small, supportive reminders that even the high and mighty face the same transition, sometimes in extremely unexpected ways, like Prince, and sometimes in luckily forewarned ways, like Bowie.

Within days after Tracy died Fugen set me up with an MKP man in New York who had lost his own wife five months to the day before Tracy. She too was only in her 50s; she too had cancer. Given his head start, I looked to Stan for leadership in walking this painful path. We became grief buddies, talking every other week, eventually coming to mentor each other. Then I learned my old China friend David Engle was dying at 67. Following his death I turned to offer what little I could in support of his widow and oldest son—all of them, including their daughter, dear to me. Then Thanksgiving day came and I was reminded how Tracy's sister's husband had died from brain cancer on that day only a year before. Another good man, dead too soon.

For the first four months, it seemed that everywhere I turned was death. Someone recently dead, somebody dying, some already forgotten. The story of the mustard seed from the Buddha's life sprang to mind. A mother lost her young son. She came to the Buddha and pleaded with him to bring him back to life. Other versions of the story say she pleaded to be relieved of her suffering. In any case, the Buddha said, "Yes, I can do that. But first you must bring me a mustard seed from a home where no one has faced a similar loss." So the woman set out. She went from home to home, knocking on doors and inquiring. It seemed everywhere she went someone in each family had suffered a terrible loss...fathers, daughters, uncles, mothers, friends...Everyone knew the heartbreaking loss of someone beloved. She couldn't find a soul who hadn't experienced some devastating pain like hers. In this way she healed the pain from her own loss, and in keeping with the first scenario, realized that despite her great love, there was nothing unique enough about her son to merit his resurrection above all other beings.

I love this story. It illustrates a number of dharma themes I hold most dear. Suffering is the most common gateway to undertaking appreciation and study of the teachings. It opens the heart and invites compassion of self and others. Everything is impermanent; nothing lasts. Not love, not relationships, not people. We live under the illusion that our individual suffering is unique. Yet the Buddha made very clear in his First Noble Truth that suffering is universal and absolute. Furthermore, we are interdependent. What you do affects me and vice versa. Who's to say who healed whom when the grieving mother made her rounds? Yes, her grief was lessened when pooled with the grief of strangers she met. But how might *she* have helped them with their losses?

The story also illustrates the maxim that only the broken hearted can effectively support the heartbroken. Though not a dharma theme per se, it's certainly what I have found to be true. Again and again I'm drawn to the company of the grief-stricken, all the spouses and friends who lost someone beloved. We understand the depth of each other's pain and need not explain or falsely bandage. We suffer; we share; it's real. In a strange, perhaps shadowy way, I feel like I need to break everyone's heart with my story so I know there are people I can stand together with. Though I weep and tremble at the stories of pain I've encountered, I have nothing but gratitude for the mysterious workings of a universe that sees fit to usher other grievers into my company.

Another axiom I've come to know: even when our most beloved dies we say to ourselves "Gee, I'm glad it's not me." The response may not be admirable, but it's real. Saying otherwise is romantic hogwash. Though there were plenty of times I would gladly have taken Tracy's pain on myself if it would have reduced hers, I never once sincerely wished I was dying instead of her. Unless and until it comes after a long period of suffering with no end in sight, no one really wants to die. Even those crazed with suicidal ideation like me. The dying understand this better than most. They consider it an affront to their own reality to have others neurotically moan about dying when it's not happening to them; it's not their reality. Not yet. The dying want to see others live most fully, to claim their aliveness, their birthright to embody life force. Those not in denial or clinging to their neuroses while dying are actually reassured by this, tasting that aliveness to their last breath. That's what Tracy did.

Right now in my office I'm increasingly surrounded by images of the dead. Taped to my computer I have a photo of Tracy and one of my Mom and Dad at my Dad's Ph.D. graduation. Over my desk I have another photo, more recent, of my Mom, and one of old family friend Steve Schultz, born April 14, 1953, died 1996. They say this happens as a function of getting older, that the dead increasingly encircle you. For me, it's been a function of my life since the beginning. I've lost friends and family in every phase of my life, perhaps even every year. Beloved soul Steve Schultz died of AIDS. His sweet and gentle partner Don died of the same illness five years prior. Chuck Gainey and Larry Vaughan, two beloved Southern Illinois farmer-neighbors, also my age, also died of AIDS. I can count at least 50 people off the top of my head who were either friends or family who have died, most of whom are not my parents' generation...Is this normal? It seems like a lot of death to me. It makes me miss one aspect of the gongyo ceremony, the recitation of the sutras, as taught to me by the SGI. Every day we'd sit in silence and ring bells to honor the dead. Even then, in my early 30s, I was struck by how long my list was. Simply remembering all my dead friends and family was a challenge. Over the passing years such accounting has become unmanageable. Yet there's something about honoring the dead that feels essential, even sacred, to the meaningful working of our lives, nowhere better evidenced than in James Joyce's *The Dead*:

> *A few light taps upon the pane made him turn to the window. It had begun to snow again. He watched sleepily the flakes, silver and dark, falling obliquely against the lamplight. The time had come for him to set out on his journey westward. Yes, the newspapers were right: snow was general all over Ireland. It was falling on every part of the dark central plain, on the treeless hills, on the Bog of Allen and, farther westward, softly falling into the dark mutinous Shannon waves. It was falling, too, upon every part of the lonely churchyard on the hill where Michael Furey lay buried. It lay thickly drifted on the crooked crosses and headstones, on the spears of the little gate, on the barren thorns. His soul swooned slowly as he heard the snow falling faintly through the universe and faintly falling, like the descent of their last end, upon all the living and the dead.*[6]

[At the recommendation of my grief buddy Stan, I tried "talking" to "Tracy" after she died. He'd been "talking" to his "wife" quite regularly for some months since her death. One

---

6. The final paragraph from Joyce's THE DEAD—for me, the greatest short story in the English language.

month after she died, I took out my Journal and began writing... Here it is, verbatim.]

August 11

I hereby invoke the spirit and presence of Tracy, so that I may continue to commune with her in this changed state. Please Tracy, stay close to me. I need you. Let this imaginative dialogue be a success. I want you near, Tracy. I want your wisdom and your counsel and your goodness.

Me: Tracy, my love, are you there?

Tracy: Yes.

Me: I love you and miss you so much!

Tracy: I love you too.

Me: How are you now sweetheart?

Tracy: At peace.

Me: Really?

Tracy: Yes. How can I be of most help to you?

Me: I know and I don't know. There are many ways but I feel they're too insignificant.

Tracy: What are they?

Me: I need money for my film. I need help with your daughters. I need help dealing with my horniness. I don't need help letting go of you. I don't want to. I like writing about you every day. Though reading over this journal makes me too sad. How can I best keep you close?

Tracy: You're doing it. Kiss my ring. Anything else?

Me: Not really. I mostly want to know you're near, to feel you near.

Tracy: Keep writing.

> Me: You would say that!
>
> Tracy: Of course!
>
> Me: I love you so much.
>
> Tracy: I love you too.
>
> Me: Why couldn't I go with you?
>
> Tracy: It's not your time.
>
> Me: I apologize for not making love with you more often.
>
> Tracy: It is sad but it's done. Anything else?
>
> Me: You remind me now of when you were focused on work, not wanting to be bothered or distracted.
>
> Tracy: It's different now. Are we finished?
>
> Me: I guess so. But I don't feel happy.
>
> Tracy: You will. Again.
>
> Me: Will you?
>
> Tracy: I am. Good night.

The conversation, if that's what it was, wasn't a satisfying experience. The skeptic in me prevailed. How do I know that what is coming through me is her and not 100% projection? I suppose I could've asked for some unmistakable sign. But what's "unmistakable?" Everything I wrote is exactly what I imagine she would say. There was nothing there that surprised me or felt revelatory.

But more so I felt like even if it was all "real," I was intruding on her experience. Does she want or need me to have these conversations with her now? This is an expression of *my* needs. Do I have to come first even now, in her death? Can't I just leave her in peace? I didn't attempt it again.

I frequently wonder what my last dying thoughts will be. In dry runs, I'll cast my mind over life events, lightly, hoping that it might come to rest in good places. I hope to be reminded of some small but singular event I'd forgotten. I hope I might discover in myself a long forgotten moment of great kindness and tenderness. Of course when the actual time comes, there might well be surprises. Random events that had no significance when they occurred and have none while dying. A final spin of the mind's roulette wheel—red, black, odd, even—it might all be random, no landing place especially meaningful. One more thing to be fearful of.

When I rehearse now usually it comes to rest on bookends: moments when I first met someone, moments when I saw their face one last time. Of course, accompanying these are the feelings: the hope, often nervous and expectant, and the inevitable sadness, always the sadness, from loss—missed opportunities, forgotten connections, the deaths, despairs, postmortems…children unhugged, coaches unthanked, mentors unacknowledged, betrayers not told off, shadowy figures not challenged, social protests unengaged.

Who will accompany me on my death journey like I accompanied Tracy? That's what I really want to know. I don't want to die alone. I don't want to die solely in the company of friends and family. I'd like to die with a soul mate, my beloved by my side. Perhaps it's selfish or romantic or grasping. But I'd like to leave this world with the absolute total acceptance and caring with which I believe I entered it, with the love of my father and mother. I believe that's how Tracy felt when she left. That level of trust is unsurpassed. I want it too. So one of my new lifetime goals is eventually to find a partner who will walk those final steps with me. No doubt a strange position for which to review applicants.

It's easy to trot out clichés and say, "Oh, Tracy would want you to be happy. She'd want you to have lovers again." Nobody knows. What I do know is that the subject was painful whenever we drew near it. She did comment that widowers tend to receive high marks from potential partners. But the thought of me with another woman always brought her distress and grief. Certainly I'm going on with my life and I'm going to have other lovers. But I'm not going to pretend it's somehow making her happy in the beyond.

Before I had my first post Tracy lover spend the night with me, sleep in the bed that I bought with Tracy and that was ours to share, and stay the night in the bedroom where I still have an altar for Tracy six months after she died, I did a ceremony at that altar requesting her permission and approval. Mostly, I made it clear that I in no way intended any disrespect. "I'm just a schmuck with physical and emotional needs," I said. I imagine people might read this and say, "After only six months! What a cad!" I confessed to "Tracy" that, as usual, I don't know what I'm doing. I'm just stumbling through life making the best decisions I can in each moment. I've always been a failure at living up to others' expectations. To open my heart to another woman, to make love again, to not preserve our bedroom as some inviolable shrine, forever to be inhabited by me alone, seems like a reasonable decision to me. Still, I miss her, love her, and honor her memory. Crying at the altar, I spoke a modified version of the Mourner's Kaddish, the Jewish prayer for the dead:

At the rising of the sun and its going down I remember you.

At the blowing of the wind and in the chill of winter (and boy has it been cold!) I remember you.

At the opening of the buds, in the rebirth of spring I remember you.

At the rustling of leaves and in the beauty of autumn I remember you.

At the beginning of the year and when it rains (and boy has it been raining; you would've loved it.) I remember you.

As long as I live, you too shall live: For you are now a part of me, as I remember you.

When I am very weary and in need of strength I remember you.

When I am lost and sick of heart. I remember you.

When I have joy I crave to share I remember you.

When I have decisions that are difficult to make. I remember you.

When I have achievements that are based on yours I remember you.

As long as I live, you too shall live: For you are now a part of me, as I remember you.

And I should add:

Even as I date and sleep with other women I remember you.

CHAPTER 9
WALKING HALLWAYS

TOMORROW IS MY 61ST birthday. I'd rather have someone stomp on my foot. How many more birthdays do I have to face without her? She witnessed and supported me through the high drama I created around my 60TH birthday, beginning when I was about 58½. We didn't usually make a big deal out of birthdays but she was the actual cause of my eventual hometown debauch. She kept asking me "What do you want to do for your 60TH?" My deadpan answer was always, "Is suicide an option?" This was during the long period of my depression. Since the prospect filled me with nothing but dread I put off giving her a direct response for at least a year.

Those big birthdays are built-in self-examination tools. Like it or not, you're probably going to ask yourself, "This is it? This is all that I've managed to do with my life?" If you're like me you're most likely going to come up short. "Yep, that's it! That's all you've done! Deal with it." It was that build-up to my 60TH that convinced me to begin a new strategy for my life: acknowledge failure privately to myself then declare victory to the world and move on. My list of failures is long. Hence, my list of victories is growing.

I finally realized I could inflict myself on my old, best friends facing the same wretched crossing. I'm a lifetime believer in the maxim *misery loves company*. I figured if I have to face turning 60 as a failure I'd like to do it with my two oldest friends who were also turning 60. David was my best friend when I was 13 and Ben since 14. We had almost 50 years of connection to provide fertile ground for shared commiseration. Though far from failures themselves, I thought if they're not plagued by the same thoughts they'll at least accept mine. They're certainly used to hearing me complain.

That was the original plan. But then it grew. Though ostensibly restricted to the two classes that contained the greatest number of people turning 60, before long it became an open invitation to pretty much anyone in our high school. I'm guessing about 40 people turned up in the large and beautiful home that David shares with his wife Janet—a graduate from the class ahead of us, also turning 60. This from a small school where the average graduating class only has about 40 students.

Turned out to be a hell of a lot of fun. My sole guiding directive was no bullshit. Be real. About your fears, your regrets, your failures. Call me Jewish, but I have an abiding belief that if you begin from a place grounded in the suffering that's present for you, you'll soon find yourself sharing belly laughs, making toasts, and rediscovering that as long as you can have evenings like this then maybe things aren't so bad after all. I only know one direction—through the pain. There's no sidestepping it.

You live long enough and all your heroes die. Many of the people I loved and admired in my youth and early adulthood are already gone: Andrei Tarkovsky, Phil Ochs, Kurt Vonnegut, Bayard Rustin, Akira Kurosawa, Lenny Bruce, Huey Newton, George Jackson, Allen Ginsberg, John Lennon, George Harrison, Vaclav Havel, Wilt Chamberlain, Muhammad Ali, Saul Alinsky, I.F. Stone, Luis Bunuel, Jim Harrison, Richard Pryor, Michelangelo Antonioni, John Berger, Leonard Cohen. Even your contemporaries start to go: Bruce Sinofsky comes right to mind, from diabetes no less. One rudimentary marker of the length of your life is how many years you've outlived the greatest number of your own luminaries.

Now as I write this my 61ST birthday is here. Despite my not wanting it, come it did. And despite all my advance anguish, it turned out pretty well. On retreat at Dai Bosatsu Zendo (DBZ), I seized the opportunity during a morning staff meeting to let it be known. I said, "I don't need anything from you. I just want you to know today's my birthday and to please hold the thought with me because this is the first birthday I've had in 13 years without my wife." Life goes on even when we don't want it to. Death or another day; that's often the simple choice. It's all too tempting to choose death. But when I choose life unexpected things sometimes happen.

Tozan drove Sosan and me into the tiny town of Roscoe. We went to Raimondo's—a nice, family-run Italian place, with real Italians. We listened to the Rat Pack hit parade—Sinatra, Martin, et al, which sounded heavenly, and had a great lunch. Then we spread out and went to work, availing ourselves of wifi. Mostly though, I read birthday greetings from 150 people. We watched kids come in dressed in their costumes, getting candy. We flirted with the cute waitresses, one dressed in a hot cat outfit. In response to all the good wishes, I posted a photo on my page from 2014 of Tracy at Rochester Airport. We had run across a kids play zone while waiting for our plane. I asked her to get in. She played the part with real exuberance and joy, a kid really thrilled to be taking off in a jet plane, amply demonstrating her willingness to throw herself fully into any moment, making it a festival.

All the quotidian tasks of monastery life—and there are many, absolutely constant cleaning being the main one—are made psychologically so much simpler because there are no alternatives. I can't kick back in front of the tube with a beer. I can't jerk off watching porn. You're committed to a certain period of time there. It will not serve you to ruminate about life elsewhere, not for a single moment. In a strict sense it's similar to prison. Nowhere to go, nothing to do. Unlike prison, it's quiet, and relatively easy to achieve a mindset of equanimity. Monastery, prison, daily life... we're all doing time.

But it's not so easy to maintain equanimity once out. Doing exactly the same tasks at home is made much harder because of the multitude of other options that always exist. Why clean the stove? I can have the cleaning lady do it on Wednesday. "Look at all these dirty dishes my guest left... Couldn't he clean up after himself? What the hell?" And so the grousing continues... All the practice in the world, even for great periods of time in the most remote retreat centers, won't necessarily mean a goddamn thing when it comes to practicing outside those walls. Moments of joy can be truly fleeting but fortunately moments of anguish can too.

Now as I write this it's New Year's Eve. Yes, time is passing quickly, too quickly. Soon it will be six months since her death. I want time to slow down. It's the opposite of what I felt in the first months following her death. The excruciating pain then was intolerable. "If time would only move faster perhaps the pain would recede more quickly." Now that extreme pain is itself becoming a memory. There is increasing joy and ease in its place. But there is also that accelerating pace. The carcinogen free, environmentally sound frying pan she bought now has permanent stains, perhaps from my inappropriate use. Yesterday, I took the earbuds off her nightstand that have been there since she died because mine are falling apart. I tried repurposing her battery powered bedside clock to use in the bathroom but it hasn't worked properly since she died so I threw it out. The big Chinese fan she put in front of Beanie's cat box in the hallway is already in tatters. I tossed that too. Our landlord has sold the building and the time may soon come when I have to move. It's irrelevant to him and future buyers that she died here, even though for me it's sacred ground.

And as time speeds up, accumulating past her death, I'm starting to forget her. What her cheek felt like on mine, what my fingers felt running through her hair, the firm and rounded tones of her speech, what it's like to roll over and find her in bed, the exact words and tone of her response when I let her know "Honey, I'm home!" The relentless pull of time takes her further away from me every day. It's not like I have a choice whether to stay fixed in that stream or not. I am in that stream, part of that stream; I can't stay stationary. So I feel the water rushing around me, over me, through me, washing me clear of grasping, of memory, of all that I knew about her and our exquisite life together. Unless I die first, eventually too Beanie will die, and with her the last living, everyday reminder of our life together will perish. Time moves me not only further and further away from her, but faster and faster.

I'll be eating lunch or brushing my teeth when I'll remember some choice bit about her. I'll rush back to my computer to record it before it leaves my memory again, like some squirrel returning to its nest with a prized nut for the winter. I'm not sure what this says about me other than I'm still driven by fear. How much will I forget? So many golden nuggets already washed away…

This process also brings home to me how much I might have missed in our relationship. How many moments I truly didn't notice or savor. What is this very record if not partly an unintentional compendium of my unconsciousness? A permanent record of my obliviousness to some of her many wonders? Too much of what I've remembered has only underscored how dismissive and inattentive I was to many of her charms.

I don't trust people who say they don't have regrets. Strikes me as bullshit, macho posturing. How can you not have regrets? Have you learned nothing from your life? That's what regret signifies. All the times you did something stupid, that you wish you could do over, or times that you did nothing when you know you should have intervened, they're part of the continuum on which we measure our growth. I have plenty of regrets. The time at the Editors Guild ceremony that I publicly embarrassed James Cameron for his pronunciation of my colleague's name. The time that I decided to reenact Marty Feldman's "walk this way" moment of hunchback hilarity from *Young Frankenstein* in front of a group of colleagues that included a man with a hunchback. And it's not just moments of clear embarrassment or shame. Like the last fight I had with Tracy. Would it have killed me to simply say I'm sorry and be done with it even if I didn't feel like I had anything to be sorry about? There have been numerous small miscalculations too, when a simple word or gesture of kindness could have made a definitive difference, shifting the calibration of an entire relationship. All the times in the years building up to our final one together that I passed on making love with Tracy, or didn't tell her how much I loved her, expressing some indication of tenderness and care. We have but one moment to bring everything we know to the table and act decisively. This one. Depending on that choice we face the possibility of a lifetime of regret. But of course, that too is a choice. I want, especially now, to practice awareness, recognizing any wrong decision, saying "oops," marking the regret, and moving on.

The key factor is forgiveness. In the wake of these inevitable regrets can we forgive ourselves? Depending on the severity of the injury done by us or to us that's not so easy. Both are challenging for me, though I tend to find it easier to forgive others. Forgiving myself for things I've done wrong is my greatest challenge. What I call my life's greatest koan—forgiving myself for initially partnering with, then staying in relationship with Steve James to make *Hoop Dreams*, for not demanding a co-directing credit midway through the process when he reneged on our founding agreement, for not ever insisting on acknowledgment or apology, for still reverting to my childhood reflex and regularly wishing him dead, for not just slugging him in the face and being done with it—will no doubt remain my greatest challenge.

I've taken my wedding ring off. I first removed it mid-October before leaving town for a conference in Mexico. It was my first "long" trip away from home since Tracy died. I made the decision because it would be a family friendly event, where many participants bring their spouses and kids. I didn't want to answer questions about where my wife was. You could say I was being entirely practical. But left to my own devices to concoct a deeply meaningful or spiritual reason to take it off, to wait for the "right time," or to construct a ceremony around it, I likely never would have done it. Once I returned home I looked at the ring and considered putting it back on. "No, let it be," I thought. Sometimes the superficially practical reasons are the best ones. Letting timing be determined by the purely functional can be a godsend, removing us from the burden of depth. "Besides," I reasoned, "I still have *her* ring around my neck and that means a lot more to me than mine around my finger." Her ring will be much more difficult to let go.

Recently, in conversation with my financial manager for superannuation projections, I told him to posit 80 as the age of my death. That's it. 19 more years is the most I expect. Assuming I make it that far, I don't want them to go quickly. Yes, that would constitute almost a quarter of my lifetime and a lot can happen in 19 years. But it's well established that the subjective pace of life accelerates as it lengthens. I want my final years to go slowly. That's the challenge I face leading an active life. How to be busy but not hurried, how to be full but mindful.

Rummaging through Tracy's files for some tax papers I found a copy of the program from our wedding ceremony. It contained this poem from Pablo Neruda, entitled LXXXIX, which Tracy loved and insisted we include. The prescience of it rocks me.

> *When I die, I want your hands on my eyes: I want the light and wheat of your beloved hands To pass their freshness over me once more: I want to feel the softness that changed my destiny.*
>
> *I want you to live while I wait for you, asleep. I want your ears still to hear the wind, I want you To sniff the sea's aroma that we loved together, To continue to walk on the sand we walk on.*
>
> *I want what I love to continue to live, And you whom I love and sang above everything else To continue to flourish, full-flowered:*
>
> *So that you can reach everything my love directs you to,*
>
> *So that my shadow can travel along in your hair,*
>
> *So that everything can learn the reason for my song.*

I could never do justice to Tracy's life the way she could and did with her own memoir. But that certainly was much of the motivation behind my writing this book—teaching others the reason for her song.

But this is my song now. I guess it had to be this way. I have to sing it, complete with cracked notes and throat-catching sobs, replete with all my faults and foibles. I didn't want to. But this is the rite of passage the universe saw fit to offer me, to shake me from my depression, to rattle my life into some new form, to pull me from my depths and force me into some new engagement with being. Or, as Junpo likes to say, to remove my head from my rectum. Do I feel more alive? I can't say that I do, but maybe that will come. Do I feel more dynamic somehow, like I have more agency? Truthfully, no. But what I do feel is that the blood that flows through my veins somehow has more potency. Somehow the depth of the sorrow I carry has distilled and heightened the capability of each drop. Perhaps it can be of medicinal use. It might just prove to be an elixir for those similarly troubled.

> JULY 12
>
> I just came from the mortuary where I picked up Tracy's death certificate. One of the staff sought me out to tell me how heartbroken she was that Tracy had died. She was almost crying. She said they of course see dying people every day but when we were there together two months ago Tracy struck her as this luminous, exceptional being, radiating calm and goodness, even joy. The poor woman was really choked up. In a funeral home!

Today, Dec. 3, 2016, not quite five months beyond her death, I'm feeling inexpressibly close to Tracy, and insane gratitude for her presence. She did found USF's "Writing Warriors" after all. Here I am—a warrior at the Veterans Writing Group. It's a reminder to me that I need not search outside myself for signs of her—no lightning in the sky, no meadowlark landing on my shoulder to whisper "I'm here," no rock formation approximating her profile. Just do what I do, be what I am and the signs, reminders, of her goodness and love are all around me.

It's such a beautiful, warm winter day here in Santa Rosa, and I've felt joyful since waking. Starting our morning circle with silence and meditation brought me right back to Dai Bosatsu (DBZ). Even bowing as we did following everyone's check-in made me grateful for gassho and our Zen tradition of obeisance and humility to the strictness of form. I feel such tremendous gratitude and joy for the life that still is granted me. The warm breeze, the intermittent chirping of birds, the willow tree in front of me silently dancing with the wind...life is here and most present, whispering "see me, feel me...touch me, heal me." No, wait, that's "Tommy"—the Who rock opera! But it is saying "be with me now. There is no other. All that you seek is here. Stop your foolish wandering, seeking after another. I am your bride; I am the partner that you seek, and I am here." Sheesh, now I'm channeling Rumi!...I can't have my own thoughts without them running into somebody else's. Sometimes it feels as if my mind has been cannibalized, not only by pop culture but by my own free associations.

Even in my almost-moments of peace, I judge and judge and judge, judging what's good and bad, what's right and wrong, what should be and shouldn't. But if I stop judging, or more to the point, stop *believing* that my judgments add value to reality, there is no more mental confusion, no more internal distress. I really don't have to rely on judgment except in rare cases of survival; when danger is not present there is no need. I can let go of believing that there is anything real or of value in all that judging. Beyond all that judging, I simply *know*. In my deepest being my deepest knowing is always available, always ready to inform. It's the judging, the chatter, that gets in the way of the knowing. Once removed, the knowing speaks, however softly, however tremulously, saying "do this now," "do this now," do this now." I need only be quiet enough to hear what it says. I need to listen.

Now I discover that I can ride my bike past the Lake Merritt park benches we used to sit on without feeling twinges of pain. I can return from Grocery Outlet with items she would've enjoyed and feel warmth in that recognition. I can watch an episode of Colbert taking happy satisfaction in knowing she would've laughed too. Her "presence" is all around me. Not just in the places we shared during happy times but the times of death and dying too. The funeral parlor is across the street from the community center where I go for weekly yoga. Every time I walk the lake I see the building where we held her Life Honoring Celebration and her Memorial Service. I walk into Kaiser hospital regularly, where she almost died, for my own check-ups and meds. We chose these places not only because they were close to home but because dying is very much part of "being home." Death is integrated into my daily experience of life in ways that were unreachable before.

Her presence is transforming for me now. It still feels more remote than I would like, but when she arises in my thoughts it's the love and appreciation for her that arises most with them, not the feeling of loss. I'm choosing to remember her now in a different way. It's me who's keeping her "alive" rather than letting the fact of her death color and determine everything. Maybe this too is par for the course of healing, simply a function of making different choices. It's true that lightness and joy have returned to my life. I attribute it mostly to my Zen practice and to my time in the monastery. Playfulness is back. I note it with gratitude. I kid around more and find myself engaging strangers more easily, even flirting with women effortlessly when in the past I'd be hamstrung by self-consciousness and self-doubt.

If I can find Tracy anywhere it's right here in the present moment. Being fully attuned to all that is vibrant and alive around me, which is to say everything. She was so good at that. No moment was ever too small for her, too insignificant. If I can be present in all the mundane moments then I can find her. It's paradoxical. Looking closely and patiently enough at each and every moment makes it possible to experience that bubbliness, the effervescence of life. Then the aliveness in me becomes her aliveness; I can feel her. Drink Tracy Like Water. Yes. This is me, the essence of who I am. The drinker.

Most of my life I've been looking in all the wrong places—in all the big stuff, the moments of drama and deep meaning. It's certainly no flaw to seek the bottom line in everything, asking what is the essence of this moment? What are they really trying to get at? What needs to happen here? But it does have a downside. Overlooking the surface of things does an injustice to understanding the whole. It makes no sense to know the human skeleton but have little appreciation for the flush of a human cheek, the carved signature of the human hand, the fragrance of a musky perfumed woman, the sweep and roll of the crown's hair, the sparkle in the eyes. I must learn to pay absolute attention to the commonplace. The depth of focus and appreciation makes each moment resonant, makes it vital, and makes it possible to find her.

Charlotte Joko Beck, one of my newest and now favorite dharma teachers, founded a Zen school called "Ordinary Mind." That concept has been a revelation for me. We need not look outside ourselves, outside anything real that is going on, including the darkness within our own minds, our emotions and shadows, to find "enlightenment." What we seek is here all the time in the everyday, in the ordinary. In fact, that very seeking can remove us from the here and now and become its own mental framework with which to judge ourselves as insufficient. There's nothing to seek at all. Just observe and work with what's here now. Because what's here now is sufficient. It is more than sufficient; it is everything.

Ordinary mind = Extraordinary Tracy. Like petting Beanie in the morning, the time when she most needs affection. Do I love doing it because Tracy loved doing it, and did it so well? Yes. Do I do it because she asked me to do it every day after she died? Yes. But it's also about taking the time to love on Beanie because it brings *me* alive—out of the tasks of the day and into being. I can delight in her newly plush winter coat, discover the new scabs where she's overgroomed, let her tilt her head toward my hand to rub her nose and third eye, watch her lean into me to make the scratches behind her ear juicy. Now for the first time she sits on my lap regularly and keeps me company while I write. Being with Beanie I can be with Tracy. And so with almost all daily experience. Who knew that "Ordinary Mind" could accomplish what the mystical could not?

And then, when I've given up on it and least expect it, the mystical does occur, real magic arises, and the capital D Divine Mystery materializes. My longstanding dream comes true and Tracy joins me on meditation retreat. She didn't survive to see me ordained, yet here she is, in the Hollow Bones Zendo, in the January days just before ordainment, meditating, staring into the ornate circular mirror that adorns the scarred and exquisite wooden floor of this old Sonoma Mountain Zen Center barn, the mirror which is the heart of our circular sitting arrangement that's unlike all other Zen traditions. Tracy's upside down head suddenly appears just over the far rim of the mirror. *What*?! I look up and see Ashley, a young woman sitting opposite me who, although lovely herself, looks nothing like Tracy. But I glance down to the mirror again and in fact it *is* Tracy, looking much like she did when we first met, 14 years ago—same short dark hair, same glasses, same calm, steady eyes. The mirror cuts off Ashley's long hair, distorts her glasses, and lifts her gaze up. It's Tracy, younger, meditating with me! I want to bring a camera into the zendo with me so I can prove it to others. I don't know whether to laugh or cry. I'm awestruck. It's my wife. And she sits in meditation with me throughout the week. Sit after sit…sometimes her head peering out between the incense burner and the crystal lotus candle holder, sometimes eyes open, sometimes closed. Her presence is a bona fide miracle. Something I gave up seeking. Yet here it is. I'm in wonder, and tearful in gratitude.

At Fugen's recommendation, I wrote a haiku on each monthly anniversary of Tracy's death for the subsequent year. Like writing this book, like doing ceremonies at her altar and at USF, this exercise helped tremendously to continue to move the grief through my system. It somewhat marked my progress, though, like most deep emotional transitions, not in any linear fashion. In October I wrote six additional haikus as an accountability make-up for missing a meeting with him.

TRACY HAIKUS 2016–2017

AUGUST

Now it's been one month
I miss you every day
Why can't I go too?

SEPTEMBER

They say you've journeyed on
Reborn now into new life
What shape will you take?

OCTOBER

Opportunity
Collaboration coming
The future is now

My house now for sale
It's not about me is it?
Possibilities

100 days now
I fear forgetting you love
Merge soon with my soul

Life is calling me
back. Come back! We're not finished
with you yet, my friend

Women arriving...
Are they my friends, supporting?
Or want something more?

Tracy supporting
me, across the other side
She kept her promise

Still, I'd throw it all
away, give up my future
to hear her soft breath

NOVEMBER

Four months since you died.
Clinton or Trump? Who cares? Now
Sitting in ZaZen

DECEMBER

Tears still fall for you
"Seven Gifts that Cost Nothing"
You gave, now I give

JANUARY

Gone six months today.
Sesshin begins...no (know) you.
Ordination now![7]

FEBRUARY

Prayer ties burned in tears
Lakota pleas for your health
Not strong enough? Just right?

MARCH

Dating. Brushing teeth. Stool.
Habits of hygiene. Crying.
Practice to forget.

APRIL

Happy birthday love.
Your 60TH. You'd delight.
What a great elder you'd be.

MAY

A woman, now here
a Mom, sad, wise, like you, bald
She makes me happy

JUNE

No more ideas
Only loss, the gulf of time
remains. I give up.

---

7. Written *before* discovering Tracy in the mirror!

JULY

One year gone today
Not quite Bastille Day
Who's liberated?

At this one year marker, I find I'm talking to myself all the time now. I'm not sure why, or where this practice sprang from. But I recognize that it's accompanied by feelings of lightness. I'm playful, a feeling maybe akin to happiness. Not quite talking to her, but not quite not...It's just fun. I laugh more when I hear my thoughts out loud. It's easier to see them as ridiculous. I suppose it's a continuation of the practice we had when we were together. Trying out different voices and colloquialisms to amuse ourselves. I dramatize my thoughts vocally and bodily, making them sillier still. You know, "Getting jiggy with it." That was an expression Tracy loved. She used it to mean, "I agree with you." The Internet tells me it originated with a Will Smith song in 1998. Based on the context of those lyrics, I don't think she was using it correctly. Whatevs. If you haven't experienced hilarity I suggest you could do worse than start with a polished, 50ish, Caucasian English professor from Kansas widening her eyes to respond to a serious question with "I can get jiggy with it."

Where this new buoyancy will lead, I don't know. *Just float.* Maybe I can become the latest Monty Python Minister of Silly Walks. Tracy always commented on how we were similarly easily amused. This is a good trait to have. Seems entirely possible as long as I'm fiercely unwilling to take myself seriously.

There often comes a time during our Hollow Bones Retreats when one person starts laughing uncontrollably. Amazing how infectious truly heartfelt laughter is. If anyone comments at all it's usually "He finally got the joke." The joke being how ridiculous it is to try to control anything; to experience whatever arises with anything other than total acceptance...the simple absurdity of so much human grasping. We have moments when the entire zendo disintegrates into merriment, bodies sprawled across zabutons, shaking and howling with delight. Occasionally these moments are spontaneous. More often they're constructed through a ritual we call "Sacred Laughter." We recall moments in our lives when we've been emotionally stuck. In anger, fear, shame, sadness...the emotions and circumstances don't matter. Then, with a slight shift in perspective toward our wisdom mind, our heartfelt mind, our pure discernment mind, we "spontaneously" see it clearly for the misguided folly that it is and laugh our asses off. It doesn't take much. Just a willingness to let go of "the way things should be." Junpo always says, "To experience delight just turn on da light."

Tracy delighted in so many things. My new goal in life is to become as mirthful as she was. Laughter is the key antidote to my anger, my fear, my suffering, all my neuroses. You'd never know it from this book, or from most of my films, but I used to think that was my real purpose for living. Certainly saying, "I was born to create comedy," usually gets a laugh. My most secret aspiration, my most grandiose ambition from my early adult years after I first discovered filmmaking, was to some day make films that had a smattering of the impact, the pathos and the humor, of Charlie Chaplin. Since I failed, I'm herewith declaring success.

Buddhists of many different persuasions say that to be born into a human life is a gift of immeasurable proportion. That every human life presents an opportunity to return to oneness (or God, if you prefer), not after you've lived, but while. Each of us represents an unlimited capacity for joy, creativity, and service to the greater good. My single greatest fear in life has always been that my final thought will be, "I blew it. I wasted my life. I could've done so much more..." I pray that that was not my father's last thought. I feel confident it was not Tracy's. I want to leave this life knowing I realized my greatest potential, maximized my every opportunity, wasting not a precious breath.

My father's sudden death began my obsession with dying and generated numerous accompanying neuroses—my suicidal ideation, my expectation that death is the logical end of every conflict, my fantasies of murdering my enemies, my fixation with dying, my assumption that I'll lose all my loved ones to sudden death. It may also have generated much of my depression and despair. Tracy's death relieved those fears and suspended many of those neuroses. Death is no longer some unnamed Other, some force of darkness and confusion. It's not a manifestation of evil. It's not an occasional interloper, here to do me harm. It's with me all the time. Most surprising to say, it is not my enemy; it is a companion—still mysterious, yes, but a known, familiar escort far more recognizable, far more trusted and intimate, here to lift blinders from my eyes, to present truth, to awaken me. I know now, in its presence, in walking with death, as I did with Tracy her final months, there can be comfort and ease, moments of immense beauty and wonder, a depth of sharing, an experience of love and devotion I'd not thought possible.

There's a famous story kicking around Buddhist land. Like most, it has multiple versions. I'll relate the Zen version, starring, of course, a Zen Master. Out walking one day, our Zen Master is confronted by a ferocious, man-eating tiger. He slowly backs away from the animal, only to find that he is trapped at the edge of a high cliff; the tiger snarls with hunger, and pursues the Master. His only hope of escape is to suspend himself over the abyss by holding onto a vine that grows at its edge. As the Master dangles from the cliff, two mice—one white and one black—begin to gnaw on the vine. If he climbs back up, the tiger will surely devour him, if he stays, then there is the certain death of a long fall onto jagged rocks. (Some versions say other tigers wait below.) The slender vine begins to give way, and death is imminent. Just then the precariously suspended Zen Master notices a wild ripe strawberry growing along the cliff's edge. He plucks the succulent berry and pops it in his mouth. His final thought? "How delicious!"

In the end we're all forgotten. This is the way of things. Only very few names stand the test of history. John Mellencamp, a songwriter and musician of middling talents, recently lamented this publicly when he compared himself to Bob Dylan, recognizing that Dylan alone will be remembered from this era. Yes. The best we might hope for are practices that commemorate and honor dead ancestors—the dead ancestors we'll all soon enough be—like commonplace rituals observed every day in Japan. We all stand on the shoulders of our grandfathers and grandmothers. The lives we lead are in many ways products of the dreams they had for our lives—the self-sacrifice and devotion. The cultural practices they leave for us are their bequest too. Mentorship, rites of passage, values, rituals, myths and stories, morals and ethics…these are the gifts of the past enriching our human birthright. Our task in our lifetime is simply to recognize and honor them, perhaps tweaking them slightly before blessing them on their way, furthering their advance through time.

I still miss her. Though I don't say it to myself every day I still say it often enough. "Tracy's dead." And there are many times that I still can't grasp it at first. Why is it still true? Why can't I just be wrong? Won't I hear her coming round the corner carrying fresh vegetables from the morning market? Half-smiling mischievously when she finishes a tale about some new administrative blunder saying, "That's crazy talk!" Usually thoughts like these signal only thing. Time for another round of tears. That's all I know how to do. Weep, weep, and weep some more. Every time I think I've hit bottom—"This has got to be the end"—another round awaits. The difference now is that the gaps are greater and the depths of the internal squeezing are lessened. I've gone whole months without tears. Happy. But more importantly, tranquil.

According to Laurie Anderson in her otherwise sublime film *Heart of a Dog*, Tibetans believe you should never cry when you lose a loved one. They say that you disturb the transition of the dead through the bardo, perhaps confusing them, suggesting to them that they shouldn't move on to their next life. I'm sorry. That's crazy talk. I'm a human being. Very much full of all that life offers me. Full of shit sometimes, yes. But full of tears from a broken heart. This is part of what makes us human. I have no desire to be "perfect" and conform my life to some philosophy or set of standards, however exalted. Life itself is my teacher. It tells me that when my beloved dies, weeping is entirely appropriate. Instead of the Tibetan edict "don't cry," which sounds like a highfalutin form of emotional repression, I prefer the words of Rabbi Robert Kahn: *Tears are the proof of life. The more love, the more tears. If this be true, then how could we ever ask that the pain cease altogether. For then the memory of love would go with it. The pain of grief is the price we pay for love...We have a scar for the rest of our lives.*

I close now with this photo of Tracy and me at our wedding. Not because she was so beautiful and happy, even though she was, not because this is how I want to remember her, even though it is, not even because this was the happiest day of my life, but because it vibrates with the energy and animating force that is life itself... In the end it is not death that is any way remarkable but the fact that we have lived, and lived well. It is in our living that we should vie to be remembered, albeit with our hopefully peaceful and happy deaths as part of the fullness of that living. May we each bow to the divinity that is life, and to its most human expression in each and every one of us. And in equal measure may we bow to death, that which is the home from which we all come and to which we all return.

In her last few weeks Tracy would get up in the middle of the night, go sit at the kitchen table, fall asleep, wake up, and come back to bed. Stumbling through the hall in the dark she twice stepped on Beanie, setting her off yowling. I couldn't understand why she was doing this. Where is she going? What is she trying to accomplish? It's life, I finally decided. Her life force. That pure, unadulterated part of her that knows she's dying but still has energy to burn, that still wants so much to live. She knows there are things still to be done, that she'd like to do. That inviolable energy was enough to get her to the kitchen table, the place of work. But that was all she had. Once there, nothing remained for her to do anything with. She told me at those times she saw people in the house, specters, also walking the hallway. I said, "It's the ancestors, coming to escort you home." She nodded her agreement. Maybe I'll see them too when it's my time and maybe one of them will be Tracy. Soon enough we'll all be walking hallways, looking to escort loved ones home.

THANK YOU
FOR READING MY BOOK

I HOPE YOU'VE liked *At Death Do Us Part*.

As you can tell, it was a labor of love for me to tell this story and share it with others. So it means a lot to me that you've spent this time with me.

Before you go, I have a small favor to ask:

Could you please write an Amazon review?

Even if it's only 1 or 2 sentences, your review would mean a lot to me.

Reviews are the best way for an independent book—like this one—to get noticed and reach a wider audience. For this reason, your support really does make a difference.

It's simple: Just go to this book's Amazon page, scroll down, and click "Write a customer review."

So please take one minute to let others know about the value you received and what's in store for them.

Thanks again,
Frederick Marx

ACKNOWLEDGEMENTS

FIRST AND FOREMOST to the wonderful writer Liz Rosner who read early versions of the manuscript and helped me to realize it could be a book others might benefit from, advised me to make the book more about myself and my journey, helped edit it, and then helped solicit agents and publishers for me.

And to Peter Boland who printed the manuscript and filled the margins with careful line by line responses, questions about word choice, pointing out the need for additional background information and, especially, offering clarifying questions about who the audience is.

And to Lisa Wade, a supporter of both my film and writing work, who read the manuscript early and championed it in ways publicly and monetarily.

To all those many friends and contacts—though unnamed, you will not be forgotten—who connected me with agents and publishers and celebrity blurb writers, helping to make my first foray into book publishing a gentler experience.

To Austin Pierce, without whose guidance you probably wouldn't be reading this book. He created the masterful marketing campaign that put this book on the path to success.

And to Morgan James Publishing who offered to publish the book but whose insistence on removing any swear words helped clarify for me that they were not a good fit.

And to you, dear reader, for doing what no other publisher would do: believing in it, taking it to your heart, and sharing it with the world.

And yes, to Tracy, Tracy, Tracy.... This book is not even a dim second best to having you. I will say your name with praise on my lips until my last breath.

ABOUT THE AUTHOR

FREDERICK MARX IS an acclaimed Emmy and Oscar nominated filmmaker of 40 years. He is best known for the documentary, Hoop Dreams, which Roger Ebert named 'Best Film of the Decade.'

His work has been featured in: The New York Times, The Washington Post, People, USA Today, Rolling Stone, Reuters, Newsweek, US News & World Report, Time, Forbes, GQ, and The Wall Street Journal.

Marx brings fresh ideas, a unique sense of humor, and an urgent empathy to every subject he tackles. His voice is strong, clear, profoundly human, and focused on solutions.

Nearly 25 years after he attended his first meditation retreat, he became an ordained Zen priest in the Hollow Bones Order of Rinzai Zen. His recent documentary, Journey from Zanskar, was narrated by Richard Gere and featured the Dalai Lama.

Find out more about Frederick Marx and his films at www.WarriorFilms.org.

MY FINAL PRAYER

May all beings be happy.

May all beings be loved and well cared for.

May all beings live in peace and be at ease.

May all beings have sufficient food, clothing, shelter, medical care and lifelong free education.

May all beings realize their greatest potential and manifest their gifts joyfully and freely.

May all beings die with equanimity, surrounded by loved ones, knowing they lived the best life they could.

May all beings awaken to the gift of this rare and precious life, and be free.

www.ingramcontent.com/pod-product-compliance
Lightning Source LLC
Chambersburg PA
CBHW021147160426
43194CB00007B/719